Pak-Af Equation and Future of Afghanistan

Pak-Af Equation and Future of Afghanistan

Brig Vinod Anand (Retd)

Published in association with
United Service Institution of India
New Delhi

Vij Books India Pvt Ltd
Ansari Road, Daryaganj, New Delhi

Published by

Vij Books India Pvt Ltd
(Publishers, Distributors & Importers)
2/19, Ansari Road, Darya Ganj
New Delhi - 110002
Phones: 91-11-43596460, 91-11- 65449971
Fax: 91-11-47340674
e-mail : vijbooks@rediffmail.com

ISBN: 978-93-80177-39-7

Contents

Foreword

Recent developments in Afghanistan have set off alarm bells in the Indian strategic community and gains achieved over the past 8-9 years are seen at risk. Much more than at the fall of the Najibullah regime in 1992, which was in the making for years before it actually happened, this the time turn-around in fortunes has been rather sudden and almost wholly unexpected. The long-reviled Pakistani army and its rightly-maligned intelligence wing, the ISI, is now seen to have emerged as the key arbiter of the fate of not just Afghanistan, but of the politico-security situation of the region, straddling South, Central and West Asia. It is therefore the right time to understand the different scenarios that may arise and what would be the different options that India needs to consider in order to defend its national interests. Brig (Retd.) Vinod Anand, Senior Fellow at the United Service Institution has very competently taken on this task. I have gained a lot by reading this monograph and agree with most of his analysis, and this foreword is based on the monograph and my own understanding of the situation. Having lived and worked in Afghanistan for three years, studied its history, economy and current situation I have come to accept that over the next decade or so, the country will at best muddle through, one of the scenarios presented here.

Brig Anand does not see the Afghanistan situation in isolation but very correctly sites it within the complexity of equations between Afghanistan and Pakistan. India is an important part of this equation but this is another facet, much more important that many observers and policymakers mostly ignore, and that is the existential threat to itself that Pakistan sees from its western neighbour resulting largely from the unresolved issue of what is crudely referred to as Pashtunistan. The India angle is not about resolving the Kashmir issue to Pakistan's satisfaction, or withdrawing its involvement in Afghanistan's reconstruction efforts so that Pakistan does not feel threatened; such assumptions are as simplistic as they are misguided. Fundamentally, it is about the type of country Pakistan wants to become, or what its military will allow it to be. But before this is elaborated, it is important to understand internal dynamics of the Afghanistan-Pakistan relations.

President Obama, or his policy wonks, must be credited with coining the term, Af-Pak, since it correctly situates Pakistan as being both a part of the problem and hopefully of its solution. Richard Holbrooke very rightly said that even if Afghanistan had the best government delivering the governance that the country needs, there would still be no peace in that country as long as insurgents enjoyed support and sanctuary in Pakistan. President Karzai recently, to the consternation of many Indians, referred to the two countries, Afghanistan and Pakistan, as conjoined twins. What he probably left unsaid was that the two personas did not ask to be conjoined twins; being in that situation, they are condemned to live together, so they might as well arrive at a modus vivendi. In a published piece, I had described the complexity of relations between the two as one that made a spaghetti bowl look simple. Simply put, history, geography, religion and politics dictate that developments in Pakistan and actions of its strongest institution, the military, have the ability to influence the security environment of Afghanistan, and in turn be affected by it, not always with intended consequences.

The modern state of Afghanistan arose directly as a result of the desire of two empires, the British with India as its crown jewel and the Russian, fast expanding into Central Asia in search of blue water access, to avoid stepping on each other's toes that could have set off an unmanageable conflagration. Contrary to the well-accepted myths, the British were eminently successful in achieving their strategic objectives in Afghanistan in the 19th century, occasional battlefield setbacks and the loss of lives notwithstanding. The Russians were stopped at the Amu Darya (Oxus) and they could not influence developments in Afghanistan. Instead, the British were able to help establish a state with defined borders and a credible Afghan ruler, whom they subsidised with money and weapons to both hold back the Russians and not threaten India's northwest frontiers. As a price, the British held on to Afghanistan's eastern and south-eastern provinces, areas comprising Afghanistan's winter capital Peshawar, the present day Khyber Pakhtunkhwa province (erstwhile NWFP), FATA and northern Baluchistan including Quetta. The treaty between the two governing their relations and finalising the border was to last for 100 years, till 1993. In Afghan eyes the British withdrawal from India meant that the treaty lapsed, and that these lands should come back to them. Consequently, pending resolution of the issue Afghanistan was the only country to vote against Pakistan's admission to the United Nations.

Linked to this was the fact that Jinnah and his Muslim League was weak in NWFP, where the Congress had won the provincial elections in 1946, a reflection of the success of Ghaffar Khan's secular Khudai Khidmatgar movement. NWFP reluctant went to Pakistan as its two preferred options, a unified India or merger with Afghanistan were not on offer. Daud Khan as Prime Minister of Afghanistan (1953-63) raised the banner of Pashtunistan but could not really force the issue, ultimately lost his job as Pakistan's economic blockade was too steep a price for Afghanistan to pay; Pakistan became an American ally by joining SEATO and CENTO and Afghanistan, as a non-aligned country increasingly got financial, political and military support from Russia. Brig Anand rightly reminds us that Zulfiqar Bhutto's government gave shelter to two important Afghan rebels, Rabbani and Hekmatyar, and tried to facilitate uprising in Afghanistan, the first of Pakistan's adventurist forward policy in that country.

Ultimately, it was the Russian armed intervention that made Pakistan the supreme arbiter of which Afghan jihadi group to favour with foreign monetary and military support. Zia, who was in the international dog-house after his military coup and judicial murder of Bhutto, now became a darling of the west, the bulwark of the free world against the godless communists, who could dictate terms of the assistance that he wanted for himself and for the Afghans. Obviously, the jihadi groups that were subservient to Pakistan's interests were the biggest gainers. The jihad had its repercussions in Pakistan as well. It enabled, Zia, not only to accelerate the process of *Islamisation* of the army, it also weakened Pashtun nationalism by making Islam the dominant theme in Pashtun politics. In the bargain, dominant, secular and nationalist political parties like the National Awami Party became sidelined. The story of how the failure of the jihadis to run a coherent government in Afghanistan post-Najibullah and the resultant rise of the Taliban to power with Pakistan's strong material support is too well known to be repeated.

Where does India come into the Afghanistan-Pakistan equation? Firstly, it is not by choice as India has not seen Afghanistan as a battlefield where Pakistan must be confronted. In fact, when Afghanistan-Pakistan relations were tense in the 1950s, India was hardly of any support to the Afghans. The Afghans looked to the US, and having failed to get assurances that in the event of an attack from Pakistan, they could get support, they turned largely to the USSR. However, a plural, non-aligned Afghanistan where Islam was not a political issue on its western borders having good relations with democratic, secular and non-aligned India on its eastern border unsettled the Pakistani army. Therefore, Pakistan's geographical position of lying between the two countries became an asset used to foil the development of close economic ties between Afghanistan and India. That Afghanistan is a land-locked country with Pakistan (then) providing its only access to the world for its imports and exports was used to the full by Pakistan to constrain Afghanistan developments. Post-2001, Afghanistan's request to India to build the Zaranj-Delaram road and help develop Iran's Chabahar port as an alternative to access through Pakistan must be seen in this light. Taliban's focussed targeting of the construction of this road and now movement on it is confirmation of their relationship with Pakistani army.

Secondly, a failed state or a client regime in Kabul, gives the Pakistani army 'space' where jihadi groups get sanctuary, run their camps and organise their activities. Pre-2001, large number of camps for jihadis jihadis operated in Afghanistan. When the Americans lobbed cruise missiles on Osama's camp after the attack on American Embassies in East Africa, it killed scores of jiahdi being trained for operations in Kashmir. That Kandahar was the final destination of IC-814 was not coincidental. India's stake in a stable and secure Afghanistan is real, even as the Pakistan's army would have it otherwise.

Thirdly, the misguided perception of Afghanistan affording Pakistan 'strategic depth' against India is an inversion of theory and of history. The space between the Russian borders and its hinterland allowed the Russian army to keep withdrawing before Napoleon's invading army leaving a scorched earth behind. Does the Pakistan army's strategic plans envisage a withdrawal to the Hindu Kush were the Indian army to cross the border? Possibly the Pakistani army sells this idea of strategic depth more a PR exercise to mislead its own people and the West as justification for its adventurist Afghan policy? General Kayani's recent statement on his expectations of what the Afghan army should look like – it should not pose a threat to Pakistan, it should be trained by Pakistan etc – suggests a subtle variation of this argument.

Lastly, the Pakistani army has an 'India' fixation that prevents it 'accepting asymmetries in size and capability'.[1] Something that it

---

[1] Phrase used by Foreign Secretary Nirupama Rao, speaking at a track II meeting at Shimla, June 13, 2010.

would like Afghanistan to accept vis-à-vis itself! One the one hand, it seems programmed to portray an India hand whenever its objectives are thwarted. On the other, this also suits its corporate goals to paint India as a villain and a threat without which it would not be able to dominate the Pakistani landscape and appropriate an inordinate share of the country's resources. In fact, from the time of its creation, the Pakistani elite has raised this bogey and, according to Husain Haqqani, without it, and its related aspect of Islam in danger, there's nothing else that justifies the creation and continuance of Pakistan as a State.

There are also other stakeholders which have an important role to play in stabilising the Afghan situation, or in influencing future developments in that country. This would also affect India's choices. The most prominent of them is the United States. Its reliance on the Pakistani army, with all the ups and downs, is now fairly well known. Musharraf was able, like Zia before him, in converting an adverse situation to his advantage by sufficiently collaborating with the US' war on terror. Far from seeing his country 'bombed back to the stone ages', Pakistan became the preferred partner both for geographic and tactical reasons – the Americans could not really access Afghanistan but through Pakistan, and the Pakistani army was the key to eliminating Al-Qaeda. In the bargain, Pakistan got unprecedented foreign assistance, many times what war-ravaged Afghanistan could even dream of, which enabled the Pakistani economy to grow quite impressively for the next 4-5 years. More importantly, it allowed the Pakistani army to retain its key strategic asset, the Taliban which was enabled to slowly re-group and grow till by 2006, it posed a serious threat to the American-led Afghan nation-building and reconstruction efforts.

US officials periodically expose Pakistan for its complicit role in fermenting insurgency in Afghanistan, and sheltering all kinds of jihadis, but mostly, it is 'more carrots and less stick' that is delivered to the Pakistani army. Though both Russia and Iran were very supportive of the American role in ousting the Taliban and establishing the Afghan state, the Americans find themselves insecure in involving the Russians, and by extension the Shanghai Cooperation Organisation, in any meaningful role in Afghanistan. They also find themselves unable to engage the Iranians on account of larger West Asian concerns including upsetting its Arab allies, concerns over Iran's nuclear activities and overt support for Hamas and Hezbollah. The Americans therefore find themselves with no alternative but to rely on the Pakistani army even as it mistrusts its intentions. The Mullah Baradar incident demonstrated the lack of options in bringing the Taliban on board, even as it served as a warning to Karzai not to try and engage the Taliban directly.

The Iranian see themselves as America's strategic rivals in the region, till the latter acknowledge the former's regional primacy, particularly in the broader West Asia context. Anecdotal evidence in Afghanistan suggests a willingness within parts of the Iranian establishment to tactically collaborate with the Taliban in Afghanistan so that the American army is kept on the defensive, and Iran does not face potentially hostile action on its western and eastern borders simultaneously. Iran's rigorous crackdown on the Sunni Jundullah including the capture of its leader Rigi outside Iranian territorial limits, Pakistan's enhanced cooperation with Iran including allowing Iranian forces to carry out specific operations within Pakistan and other moves like extending support to anti-Karzai political outfits in Afghanistan points to the emerging situation in Afghanistan once the Americans leave, or scale down their operations.

The question that arises is what kind of scenario are we looking at? At present the widely accepted view is that the Pakistani army will set the agenda that would allow the US and its allies to gracefully pack their bags and declare their mission over. The ideal end-state for the Pakistani army is a stable and pliable regime in Afghanistan, discreetly controlled by the former who would have the levers of power. As long as the 'Pashtun arc' from Kunar in the Northeast to

Herat in the West via Nangrahar (Jalalabad), Paktia, Ghazni, Kandahar, Helmand and Nimroz is under their control, the Pakistani army would be comfortable with instability in the rest of the country – Kabul is problematic as it is essentially a Tajik city but bounded on three sides by Pashtun territory. In such a situation, Pakistan would continue to be Afghanistan's largest trading partner, and also its largest foreign investor. Afghanistan would revert to becoming a 'rentier' state but with Pakistan appropriating the rents.

This scenario is not a given even if it seems the most likely at present. First, there are elements in the Pakistani establishment and society who are not sold on this idea, including a number of its political elites, retired army officers and its old trading networks that operated across the region and profited from peace and normalcy. The failures of Pakistan's elected political leadership in establishing itself post-2008 elections and the continued preference of the US for treating the Pakistani army as its interlocutor has meant that Kayani and the army have managed very rapidly to re-establish Rawalpindi as the pre-eminent power centre. This is a far cry from the last year of Musharraf when he and the army were pushed to the wall and lost substantial credibility to the emerging democratic forces, e.g. lawyers movement, media etc. For various reasons, domestic as well as external, the situation could change again. 1971 and 1999 could very well be repeated.

Two, there is nothing very obvious about the ability of the Pakistani army in imposing its preferred solution to the Afghan problem. The continued ability of the different Pakistan-based jihadi groups in carrying out murderous attacks within Pakistan on religious shrines, public spaces and even military installations could both weaken the resolve of the army in setting the agenda. There is increasing evidence that the Taliban and various jihadi outfits are not all acting in concert to the tune of the army, with two broad groupings emerging. On the one hand there is the Mullah Omar-Quetta Shura and the North Waziristan based Haqqani network and the Hiz-i-Islami (Hekmatyar). On the other there is the Tehreek-i-Taliban Pakistan and assorted groupings in FATA who are fighting the Pakistan army. The latter has suffered considerable casualties, but the battle between the two seems more sporadic than sustained.

Three, all opinion polls in Afghanistan show that Pakistan is the least liked country in Afghanistan; India comes out on the top. These are the same polls that are quoted to demonstrate Karzai's loss of support, people anger at increased corruption and insecurity etc. Pakistan's pre-eminence in Afghanistan is not just likely to upset the minorities but also large sections of the Pashtuns. Afghanistan itself has undergone, and is undergoing, substantial social transformation. Close to one-third of the population has lived outside country at some time or the other. This has lead to greater public awareness of political issues and of Afghanistan's place in the world. Traditional, and even jihadi, power structures have crumbled without a viable alternative coming up. The result is an atomised structure, difficult to control and prone to instability.

The circumstances and timing of Karzai's own conversion has raised doubts on whether this represents his desperate situation, and that it is more tactical than strategic. He cannot be unaware of the fate of Najibullah, who was negotiating from his sanctuary in the UN compound, with different Taliban components just before the fall of Kabul in 1996. One cannot also ignore the prevalent world view of Afghanistan's political elite. It has reasonably clear ideas of how they would like bilateral relations between the two countries to be, based on their understanding of the ground realities, the strengths and roles of the different players and how things would shape up. There is almost universal acceptance that in the Afghanistan – Pakistan relationship, they (the Afghans) would be the junior partner, as they are militarily weaker, economically smaller, geographically challenged and less-central to the world's challenges and problems. They also accept that in such circumstances, the Afghans would have to compete for attention from the US and other international donors. There is also no thought that at any time Afghanistan, as the weaker country, would resort to the use of asymmetric warfare, as Pakistan used in Indian Punjab and Kashmir. Or, in a different way, what Pakistan is doing with its patronage of the Taliban.

In these circumstances, will Pakistan and its proxies manage to control the Afghan situation, as they could in the 1994-98 period when the Taliban was taking over the country? Again, nothing is given and all predictions will remain just predictions.

Fourthly, in this changed situation, when the horrors of mass terrorism have been experienced from 9/11 to London, Madrid, Mumbai etc, would the US and others again allow Pakistan a free run in Afghanistan? There are enough indications that the US drawdown would not mean a complete withdrawal, and the US would retain 40,000-50,000 soldiers to keep up the pressure on terrorist groups, carrying out occasional drone attacks inside Pakistan. Increasingly, there is acceptance that even if there is no de jure participation, a Pakistan-friendly regime in Kabul would not be in a position to control the whole country, and that international forces and assistance would have to continue to assist the others in the North and the West of the country.

Whether it is an Afghanistan muddling through, or whether Pakistan has a dominant role, India must explore its options realistically. A strong and secure Afghanistan is in India's interest and this is something that has been pursued since the ouster of the Taliban. Sending Indian troops in support of the American effort or to replace them is a non-starter for various reasons, least of which is because of Afghanistan's reputation as a graveyard of empires. But helping train and equip the Afghan security forces including the police is a valid option and this would be both cost-effective and relevant. However, in the immediately present scenario, it is not likely to happen but India should carry on a conversation with the Afghan establishment on this. Politically, India should engage with the full spectrum of Afghan political opinion, academia, civil society and media. Large numbers of them, including those who are sceptical of Pakistan's intentions, are convinced that it is Pakistan's insecurity vis-à-vis India that is driving its Afghan policy. Hence, they argue that India should settle the Kashmir issue so that Pakistan would stop interfering in Afghanistan. India has started engaging, rightly, with regional countries with a stake in Afghanistan's stability. National Security Advisor's discussions in China and Foreign Secretary's meetings with Iranian interlocutors are the first public indication that this is happening. Russia, the Central Asian Stans, Turkey and Saudi Arabia need to be similarly engaged. Lastly, opinions in the US and Europe are not all uniform, particularly in the former, where there considerable scepticism about Pakistan's intentions and abilities. Sharing ideas with them even as India engages in strategic dialogue with the US Administration would be in India's interest. After all, India has to live in its neighbourhood even as superpowers intervene and disengage.

30 August 2010

Shakti Sinha
(*Ex-Project Director UN Asssistance Mission in Afghanistan*)

Preface

After nine years of the current phase of war and conflict in Afghanistan that began in the wake of 9/11 terrorist attacks there seems to be no solution in sight. The tryst of Afghans commenced when the then Soviet Russia, pursuing its geopolitical interests intervened in Afghanistan in 1979. As part of the Great Game and the Cold War as well, the Afghans remained as pawns and at the receiving end. In the decades that have followed Pakistan with its own regional interests and geopolitical objectives capitalized on securing military and economic aid for itself from the Americans and the West. Pakistan's security establishment created an infrastructure of radical extremist groups that could be used to pursue its policy objectives, especially against India. It is a different matter that Pakistan is now also suffering from the blow back of such obtuse policies.

Ever since the inception of Pakistan in 1947 the leadership of Pakistan has adopted a singular military oriented and India-centric approach in its foreign and security policies. As for as Afghanistan was concerned, Pakistan's leadership objectives have been to prevent a strong Pashtun identity emerging in the region. Pashtunistan issue had also become part of the Cold War. After the withdrawal of the Soviet Union from Afghanistan and consequently the demise of the Soviet Union, the U.S. lost interest in Afghanistan. However, Pakistan continued to pursue its interests in Afghanistan through aiding and abetting the activities of jihadi groups to install a government in Kabul that would be beholden to Pakistan. During the period of the Taliban rule from 1996 to 2001 many jihadi and terrorist groups received training in Afghan camps.

This volume's first section examines Pakistan's role in Afghanistan and postulates that there has been no fundamental change in Pakistan's role in respect to Afghanistan since last six decades. Pakistan's interference in Afghanistan started in earnest in early 70s and continues till date. And it is unlikely to undergo any change in the near future despite remonstrations or pressures by the U.S. and the West. With the U.S. and coalition partners looking for an exit strategy, Pakistan has been able to make itself a key power broker in the emerging discourse. In fact, the Pentagon appears to be viewing Pakistan's ISI equation with the Taliban as something which could be of benefit, however preposterous may it seem to the Indian policy makers. Though some of the political leadership in the U.S. may harbour some doubts about the efficacy of such an approach but, apparently, the current discourse continues to be influenced by the Pentagon.

The second section looks at the dominant drivers of the current situation and gazes in the future to arrive at possible scenarios based on the trends. Unfolding and implementation of the Af-Pak strategy of Obama administration is the key driver of the likely future scenarios. The major factors which need to be taken into account are the quality of governance, strengthening of Afghan national security forces, involving the regional stake holders and improving the living conditions of the Afghan population. Weaning away those Taliban cadres who are not ideologically inclined would also be one of the considerations. Improving the socio-economic conditions and providing livelihood to Afghans besides improving the quality of justice, law and order would also be important. Above all, the international community would be required to have a sustained engagement with Afghanistan since the problems created by long years of war and conflicts are indeed complex and challenging.

Evidently, the alternative scenarios as envisioned in the second section throw open policy options for our decision makers. The scenarios have been described very briefly. A common set of implications arising out of such scenarios have been offered in the end.

I also wish to express profound gratitude to Lt. Gen. PK Singh who encouraged me to write this monograph and whose ideas and interaction provided me with balance perspective on issues related to Afghanistan. I also wish to thank Lt. Gen. Ravi Sawhney for providing me with insights on Afghan conundrum. I am also grateful to USI members and Centre for Strategic Studies and Simulation faculty who were also a great source of help and encouragement. However, I solely remain responsible for any flaws in my paper.

New Delhi *Vinod Anand*

15 August 2010

Pak-Af Equation:
Role of Pakistan in Afghanistan

"The reasonable man adapts himself to the world; the unreasonable man persists in trying to adapt the world to himself. Therefore, all progress depends on the unreasonable man".......George Bernard Shaw

Early Years

When Pakistan was created from the womb of India in 1947 it also inherited the historical baggage of the British Empire. Relations between Afghans and British rulers had never been easy. Similarly, right from its inception Pakistan and Afghanistan embarked on an antagonistic path. There were organic links between Pashtuns inhabiting on the both sides of the Durand Line artificially created by the British in pursuit of their imperialistic designs. Afghanistan a buffer state between the Russian and British empires saw recurring wars and conflicts for enhancement of respective spheres of influence by both the players in the so called 'Great Game' which continues till date in some form or the other. When British were about to depart from India, Afghanistan demanded that Pashtuns in NWFP and FATA be given a choice between independence and joining Afghanistan. Further, they also asked for a corridor through Balochistan for access to sea. At that time Indian National Congress government was in power in NWFP and there was also a demand for joining India, however impractical it was due to geographical and other factors. Afghanistan had also cast a negative vote when Pakistan's application for UN membership came up in November 1947 contending that Pakistan should not be recognized till Pashtunistan was given independence. In the coming years the relations between Pakistan and Afghanistan remained bedeviled because of Pashtunistan issue, i.e. a campaign for an independent Pashtunistan consisting of the Pashtun inhabited areas of Pakistan.

The Pashtunistan issue also became a part and parcel of the cold war. The Soviet leaders supported Afghanistan and Pashtuns in their quest based on UN principles of 'self-determination' most likely in their unhappiness with Pakistan having joined the Western alliance system. While Pakistan joined the South East Asia Treaty Organisation (SEATO) and Central Asian Treaty Organisation (CENTO) in the 50's to secure itself against a perceived Indian threat Afghanistan was viewed by the Pakistani elite to be progressively coming under the influence of Soviet block. Close and cordial relations between Afghanistan, Russia and India were viewed with concern by Pakistan. Having a friendly government in Afghanistan was a long-cherished strategic objective of Pakistan. Therefore, Pakistan did attempt to influence the Afghan government in 1973 when it granted asylum to Islamist leaders Gulbadin Hikmatyar and Burhanuddin Rabbani, who had opposed Daud Khan famous for deposing King Zahir Shah earlier[1]. Thereafter Zulfiqar Ali Bhutto the then Prime Minister of Pakistan used Rabbani and Hikmatyar to destabilize Daud's government. Thus, the tradition of destabilizing the unfriendly governments in Afghanistan through proxies had commenced much before the Soviet intervention in Afghanistan and was not a post Soviet intervention phenomenon as is generally believed. Use of proxies in the shape of *mujahedeen* or jihadi fighters, a tactic which had been resorted to against India in 1947 and 1965 was later honed

[1] Khawar Hussain, "Pakistan's Afghan Policy", Naval Post Graduate School Thesis, June 2005

to perfection by Bhutto's usurper and successor General Zia. Some attempts to improve Pakistan-Afghan relations before Bhutto was overthrown and in the initial year of Zia's regime came to naught and take over in Afghanistan by a communist regime put further pressure on Pak-Afghan relationship.

In Pakistan General Zia ul Haq appeared on the scene in 1977 after having deposed Prime Minister ZA Bhutto in a coup. Meanwhile in Afghanistan Daud Khan was overthrown by the incoming communist regime in 1978. Soviet Russia walked in at the end of 1979 to support the communist regime of Afghanistan. From December 1979 to February 1989 when Russians walked out of Afghanistan, Soviet presence there presented an existential threat to Pakistan's security interests.

Pakistan being a country based on Muslim ideology hoped to establish a common Muslim and neighborly bond with Afghanistan in pursuit of its policies and interests. Further, friendly relations between India and Afghanistan were also a cause of concern for Pakistani establishment. Perceived closeness of India with Soviet Union and its influence in Afghanistan also added to the discomfort of Pakistan. Since its inception, Pakistan's view of entire world was and is very simplistic, with the world divided between states that are considered important for their ability to provide any direct or indirect help in strengthening Pakistan against India and those that are of no help in this regard. This also required Pakistan to forge closer ties with Afghanistan but there were many difficulties in achieving a desirable relationship with Afghanistan.

Further, Pakistan government's policies of continuing to administer the Federally Administered Tribal Areas (FATA) and Provincially Administered Tribal Areas (PATA) in the erstwhile British mould prevented assimilation of these areas into settled areas. While the NWFP (including some tribal areas referred to as PATA) was made a province the tribal areas were ruled through the administrative control of the political agents who were appointed by the central government as was done during the British era. A similar pattern continued even after the partition of India.

Zia Era and Afghanistan

Having overthrown Bhutto General Zia Ul Haq chose the instrument of Islamisation to consolidate the rule of his dictatorship in Pakistan. Bhutto was hanged or one could say judicially murdered in mid-1979. Soviet Russia's incursion into Afghanistan to support the Communist regime towards the end of the same year created a geo-political disturbance to which no enduring solution could be found even after three decades of conflict. However, this geo-political situation was used as an opportunity by Zia to make itself more strategically relevant to the United States and the West. Convergence of strategic interests between the US and Pakistan then unfolded a series of events which have come back to haunt the then decision makers who supported creation of many factions of radicalized Islamist militias. This turn of events then had presented both a challenge and as well as an opportunity for Pakistan to address its long-sought security concerns vis a vis Afghanistan and if things turned more favourable advantage could also be gained against India on security issues. Supplanting of Islamic fervour to subsume the Pashtun and Baloch nationalist movement was expected to erode demands for independent Pashtunistan and Balochistan. Military aid received from the US on the pretext of fighting the Soviets and aiding mujahedeen could be used or diverted by Pakistan as it found convenient. And Zia calculated rightly that its nuclear ambitions may not be adequately scrutinized due to its cooperation with the US. Washington had in fact turned a blind eye towards Pakistan's nuclear program which had reached the capability of producing weapons by

1983. These were some of the strategic considerations behind Pakistan's Afghan policy.

Further, Pakistan became the frontline State in a long and protracted war against the atheist communists. Promotion of fundamentalist thought processes and radical Islamic ideology was expected to yield benefits at home in justifying his undemocratic rule while mujahedeen trained in Pakistan were to carry out jihad against the Russians in Afghanistan. The Americans and oil-rich Saudi Arabia were to bankroll and equip the mujahideen campaign against the evil empire. And it was under Ziaul Haq that extremism had commenced acquiring the salience that is seen in the Pakistan society now. As mentioned earlier, he patronised fundamentalism for political and ideological reasons. There was also sympathy for the Afghan Mujahideen whose struggle against the Soviets was seen as righteous. Lately, though there are some green shoots of awakening becoming visible among the Pakistani elite that these militants have turned into Frankenstein yet, the Pakistani establishment even after almost three decades of bitter experience with the radical militias are ambivalent about dealing firmly with Taliban and its off shoots.

General Zia's years of rule have also been described as the time when Islamisation of Pakistan Army and its officer corps is said to have begun in right earnest. The bonds between religious parties and Pakistan Army were increasingly strengthened during years of fighting in Afghanistan against the communists. The interaction between the fundamentalist groups, the Inter-Services Intelligence Directorate (ISI) and Pakistan Army during anti-Soviet jihad contributed in turn to reverse indoctrination of Pakistan Army. Zia had maintained that the armed forces were not only the defenders of geographical frontiers but the ideological frontiers as well. These ideological frontiers expanded beyond Afghanistan that was to later include Chechnya and Central Asia. However, all these years ISI remained committed to installing a pro-Pakistan Islamists government in Kabul. As a result, the hard liners in the ISI and the Army have been in a stronger position than ever before; and this goal has not been abandoned even now when Pakistan army is being consumed by the flame it lighted in the shape of mujahedeen and Taliban. Multiple terror attacks carried out against GHQ of Pakistan Army and other symbols of authority in October 2009 indicate the that insiders in the armed forces have provided intelligence to the attackers highlighting the degree of penetration by fundamentalist Islamists among the Pakistani forces.

The officers who were nurtured in the Islamic ambience of seventies and eighties have come of age now and have either reached the ranks two to three star Generals or are in the process of acquiring such senior ranks. It is important to put in perspective the whole notion of Islamisation and Pakistani Army as also to understand the current trends particularly relevant in the context of reticence and ambiguity shown by Pakistani Army in undertaking concerted counter insurgency operations and conclusion of deals in FATA and Swat. Shorn of political and institutional factors reluctance is predominantly based on Islamic thought of fighting with their co-religionists, howsoever misguided they maybe.

Withdrawal of Soviet Union to 9/11 Carnage

But Zia, having started the radicalization process, did not live to see the victory of mujahideen when Soviet Russia retreated from Afghanistan in February 1989 after having suffered about 13, 400 (some estimates say 14,500) dead. At the height of its presence in Afghanistan Soviet Union had deployed 150,000 (some estimates put the strength as 120,000) troops. Even though a weak Afghan communist regime led by Najibullah was placed in Kabul it soon unraveled and a succession of mujahedeen governments followed each other. (Najibullah fell in April 1992 and the first mujahideen regime commenced its rule then led by Islamic scholar Sibghatullah Mojadeddi and was soon replaced by Rabbani, under an agreement among the major parties. He became President in June 1992 with agreement that he would serve until December 1994).

Further, the democratic dispensation in Pakistan which took control after Zia's death also found it very attractive to actively interfere in Afghan internal affairs to address its geopolitical concerns. In concert with Pakistan's military security establishment and ISI Prime Minister Benazir Bhutto planned a mujahedeen operation to capture Jalalabad in March 1989. In the event the attempt to capture was a massive failure which led to the sacking of ISI chief General Hamid Gul. But the ISI as an institution remain undeterred and continued to look for alternative options.

All the time the influence of Pakistan and its ISI remained considerable. They benefited from U.S. weapons and assistance, provided through the Central Intelligence Agency (CIA) in cooperation with Pakistan's Inter-Service Intelligence directorate. The ISI gives itself the credit for organizing mujahedeen into seven major parties that in early 1989 formed a Peshawar-based "Afghan Interim Government" (AIG). Pakistan and ISI played favourites with some of the seven recognized parties. The Islamists section which was particularly favored by Pakistan was Hizb-e-Islami (the Hekmatyar party) due to its having close ties with the Pakistani Jamaat-I-Islami, both parties being predominantly influenced by radical Sunni and Wahabi ideology.

After withdrawal of Soviet Union based on Geneva Accords and thereafter collapse of the Soviet Union, Washington's interest in Afghanistan waned as it turned its attention elsewhere. Both Moscow and Washington in September 1991 agreed to a joint cutoff of military aid to the Afghan combatants. Further, there were civil-war like conditions between various mujahedeen factions and a surfeit of warlords. All the time Islamabad took pains to work for a friendly regime in Kabul especially the one which could become beholden to it.

Rise of the Taliban

Unable to achieve its goals Pakistan and ISI was looking for alternatives to continuously warring mujahedeen factions in Afghanistan. Phenomenon of Taliban had acquired certain salience by October 1994. By this time Benazir Bhutto was again back in the chair and was keen to avoid any tiffs with the military establishment and she hoped to survive longer in the office by being accommodative as far as possible to the ISI and the army. Connecting to Central Asia and improving economy were some of her ideas to make Pakistan prosperous. Before that could be achieved the Afghan puzzle had to be solved.

Bhutto's Interior Minister, Maj Gen. Naseerullah Babar, viewed the Taliban as an instrument for foisting a regime in Kabul beholden to it. In order to coordinate its assistance to the Taliban, an Afghan Cell was created in the Ministry. It is an open secret that the ISI provided transportation, fuel, communications equipment and advice to the Taliban movement. Pakistan's religious parties and clergy provided infrastructure for indoctrination and even training with the help of military instructors. Many madrassas mushroomed during this period which became nurseries for Taliban. The Jamiat-e-Ulema-e-Islam of Fazal ul Rehman, as well as the famous Akora Khattak madrassa (headed by Maulana Sami-ul-Haq) were the two main flag-bearers the Taliban's indoctrination and training.

ISI channeled the funds coming from the Gulf countries and was not beyond using the drug moneys for the noble cause of Islam.

Osama bin Laden was also been instrumental in providing funds for the Taliban. Other sources of funding were the duties imposed on trucks transiting Afghanistan from Pakistan besides smuggling, and narco-trafficking. The Taliban with considerable help from regular Pakistan army was able to take over Kabul in 1996 after a series of operations which included capture of Kandahar, Herat, Jalalabad, Kunduz and Mazar-I-Sharif as well as capturing Bamiyan in September 1998.Pakistan accorded the Taliban diplomatic recognition in end May 1997. Saudi Arabia and the United Arab Emirates followed the suit two days later. And these are the countries from where funds continue to flow even now to the Taliban for their activities.

While Taliban was on the ascendance ISI also maintained relations with Hekmatyar faction who trained and sent foreign volunteers besides Pakistanis to Kashmir[2]. ISI had been persistent with Bhutto that they needed Afghan and Arab volunteers for bleeding India and they needed sanctuary for guerilla training camps in Afghan territory. Thus ISI had some division of opinion on whom to support between Hekmatyar and Taliban but they ended up supporting both after a senior Taliban delegation visited ISI headquarters on invitation of Gen Javed Ashraf Qazi. He had replaced Javed Nasir, considered to be a rabid Islamist. Taliban demands on Pakistan in terms of funds and material continued to grow and especially of the covert kind. Benazir Bhutto during in an interview on funding of Taliban had remarked that 'It was just carte blanche'[3]. And aid in the shape of former Pakistani army officers, arms, ammunition, trucks and volunteer fighters from Pakistani madrassas poured into Afghanistan.

---

2 Steve Coll, Ghost Wars, (New York: The Penguin Press, 2004), p.290.

3 Ibid. p.291

There were reports of even regular Pakistan army officers having been sent in disguise.

The degree of involvement of Pakistan state machinery with the Taliban can be gauged from the fact that when after its nuclear tests of May 1998 it was put under punitive economic sanctions which led to financial crisis Pakistan's finance ministry authorized disbursal of 300 million rupees to the Taliban administration in Kabul[4]. This was done in a manner so that this transaction could be kept hidden from surveillance of the international community. Ahmed Rashid has very graphically recorded the arms, ammunition, spare parts for Soviet era military equipment and facilitation for Taliban to purchase equipment from Ukraine and Eastern Europe.

Return of Nawaz Sharif as Prime Minister did not make any difference to Pakistan's Afghan and Kashmir policies. The Americans continued to put pressure on the ISI and Army to facilitate capture of Osama bin Laden through their leverages with Taliban leadership including Mullah Omar. There was a great degree of skepticism amongst the CIA operatives and US Counter Terrorism officials regarding the sincerity of ISI and Pakistan Army's efforts towards helping them in apprehending Osama bin Laden. During the Kargil fiasco when Nawaz Sharif went to meet President Clinton in July 1999, he was admonished by him, "asked repeatedly for Pakistani help to bring Osama bin Laden to justice from Afghanistan- (Sharif) had promised to do so but had done nothing. Instead ISI worked with bin Laden and the Taliban to foment the terrorists."[5] Clinton called that as an outrage and threatened to release a statement regarding Pakistan's support to terrorism. In the event the threat of nuclear

---

[4] Ahmed Rashid, Taliban, Islam, Oil and the great Game in Central Asia, (London: I.B. Tauris, 2000), p.183

[5] Steve Coll, Ghost Wars, (New York: The Penguin Press, 2004), p.417

war also came up with Pakistan army having supposedly moved their nuclear tipped missiles which Clinton termed as most irresponsible, in fact crazy. Sharif buckled under this onslaught and took the decision to issue orders to the army for withdrawal from Kargil. But then he knew that this decision could lead to an army coup and which did take place in October that year.

Musharraf continued with the erstwhile policies of aiding Taliban and he perfected the art of arresting a few lower level Al Qaeda and Taliban operatives whenever the US leaders/dignitaries visited Pakistan to seek cooperation. Even though Americans saw through the game they felt that Musharraf was a guy with whom they could do business with. Whatever be the dialectics regarding the U.S. Pakistan relations leading to the 9/11 carnage the U.S. continued to defer to Pakistan in its policies towards Afghanistan. This was frustrating to many allies and friends of the U.S like Massoud of Northern Alliance whose help was eventually used to eliminate the Taliban rule in the aftermath of September 11, 2001 terrorist attacks.

Post 9/11 Promises of Strategic Transformation and Musharraf's Double Game

Once confronted with wrath of the US, Musharraf promised to reform both in its external and internal policies. Musharraf decided to join with the US in its war against terrorism, abandon its Afghan policy, condemned terrorism and envisaged Pakistan as a moderate Muslim state that would resemble more like Turkey rather than Talibanized Afghanistan. Prior to 9/11, Musharraf had been isolated at home and abroad because of his Kargil misadventure, military take over of Pakistan and failure to sustain democracy, increasing growth of religious fundamentalists and radicalism and non-investment in social and human development sectors. Pakistan was seen as a state which was floundering on the verge of being declared not only as a failed state but also a rogue state. 9/11 forced Musharraf to follow the path of 'enlightened moderation'. During his speech of September 19, 2001 he cited the following reasons for changing his strategic outlook:-

- Pakistan's strategic assets are not neutered
- Safeguarding of Pakistan's Kashmir policy
- Avoid being labeled as a rogue state helping terrorists
- Prevent an anti-Pak dispensation taking hold of power in Afghanistan
- Improve the image of Pakistan as a responsible nation

On ground, however, there was a limited effort on the part of Musharraf to change its Afghan and Kashmir policies. Pakistan's Kashmir policy came into international focus again following terrorists' attacks on October 1, 2001 and December 13, 2001 attack on Indian Parliament in New Delhi. This led to India mobilizing its forces and launching of Operation Parakram in order to force Pakistan to change its policy of cross-border terrorism. Pak president in his famous speeches of January 12, 2002 and June 2002 promised again to prevent use of Pakistan's territory by terrorists for their activities. There was little change of heart in Pakistani establishment's policies towards Pakistan and Afghanistan. In fact, after a frustrating military stand-off which was called off by India in end 2002, Pakistan was back to old ways soon.

Meanwhile when the U.S. and its allies were busy fighting second Gulf War in Iraq, Pakistan continued with its aid to Taliban and the infrastructure for providing safe haven and logistics was further developed in FATA region. Taliban renaissance began in 2004 when Pakistan Taliban started taking on the Pakistan Army. It was around this time when Afghan Taliban also started scoring successes against NATO led ISAF and American forces in Afghanistan. The causalities of foreign troops climbed dramatically to twice the number by end 2005.

In December 2004, General Karamat, Pakistan's ambassador to the US had acknowledged the misdirection of Pakistan's strategic policies and was at pain to emphasize that these have been transformed and Pakistan had to pay a price for this strategic re-orientation[6].

Ahmed Rashid a well known analyst had written in the wake of London bombings of July 7, 2005 that "*the enormous Islamic extremist infrastructure that the military maintained before September 11 to fight its wars in Taliban-controlled Afghanistan and Indian Kashmir have not been broken up, only put to temporary sleep while clandestine training camps still spring up at new locations. Some*

---

[6] General Karamat asserted that:-

(a) From a policy of active interference and destabilization of Afghanistan, Pakistan is now working with the U.S. for a stable and friendly Afghanistan.

(b) From a policy of hostility and confrontation with India, Pakistan now has a policy of dialogue and conflict resolution.

(c) From a policy of appeasement and political expediency with extremist religious elements, Pakistan has moved to confronting them to end the negative influence within the country.

(d) From a clandestine nuclear program with proliferation consequences, Pakistan has moved to a regime of command, control, and international cooperation.

(e) From vendetta-oriented political leaderships and dictatorial regimes, Pakistan is moving, slowly but surely, toward sustainable democracy and political stability.

(f) From a military-centric concept of security, Pakistan has transited to realize the importance of a broader concept of security with the emphasis on economic and internal stability. Gen. Jehangir Karamat's briefing at the Brookings Institution on December 15, 2004 titled "Pakistan-US Relations: The Next Steps The Idea of Pakistan" available at http://www.brookings.edu/comm/events/20041215.htm

militant groups have been banned three times, only to re-appear under different names"[7]. 9/11 Public Discourse Project Report of November 2005 while reviewing progress made on recommendations of 9/11 Commission Report had emphasized that Pakistan continued to be a sanctuary and training ground for terrorists and advises the US government to put pressure on Pakistan to do more to crush terrorism. Besides the terrorism in Kashmir, the Report stressed that Pakistan should act forcefully to close Taliban-linked madrassas; shut down terror camps and prevent Taliban from operating across Pakistan -Afghan border[8]. However, Musharraf continued to play the double game and the U.S. and its allies continued to praise Musharraf for his cooperation as according to the US thought process, alternatives to him could have been worse.

A replay of the cameo is again taking place under the leadership of General Kayani as reflected in Pakistan Army's operations in FATA. Kayani has been reluctant to enlarge the scope of operations to include attacks against Haqqani and other Al Qaeda linked groups taking shelter in North Waziristan. Operations in Swat, Malakand in 2009 and South Waziristan in 2010 against Tehrike Taliban Pakistan have been partially successful but that does not mean the militancy has receded in those areas.

Zardari and Gen. Kayani's Era: No Second Thoughts on Afghan Policy

Following years till Musharraf was forced out first as COAS and then later as President of Pakistan in August 2008, a bevy of US dignitaries and officials visited Pakistan to impress upon Pakistan

---

[7] Ahmed Rashid, "Nothing will change unless Musharraf closes Pakistan's militant Madrassas", South Asia Tribune, July 23, 2005

[8] 9/11 Public Discourse Project Report available at http://www.9/11pdp.org

military security establishment to change its policies on appeasement of terrorists groups as also on its selective approach towards countering terrorism. Attempts to pressurize Pakistan to deal with Quetta Shura, Jalaludin Haqqani group and Hikmetyar group which were causing immense damage to Coalition troops in Afghanistan were not successful. Coercion through linking military and economic aid to Pakistan was also not able to bring much change in military establishment's policies. With ushering in of a democratic government in February 2008 it was hoped by the international community that the new dispensation would be better able to address the challenges being posed by terrorism and radicalism and the erstwhile misdirection of Afghan policy would be corrected. The Army which had retreated to barracks after the democratic government was stalled nevertheless continued asserting its influence on Afghanistan and Kashmir policies.

Despite many testimonies by Pentagon leadership before the Senate Foreign Relations Committee about the role of Pakistan army and Musharraf's duplicitous ways in treatment of Taliban the Americans have been unable to force Pakistan to change its stance.[9] Such behaviour on the part of the U.S also gave rise to the perceptions that the US was not serious about succeeding in Afghanistan. They remained receptive to the unending Pakistani

---

[9] When General James Jones, the Supreme Allied Commander for Europe, four-star Marine general, former member of the Joint Chiefs of Staff, testified before the Senate Foreign Relations Committee on September 21, 2006 he was asked by Senator Chuck Hagel (R-NE), "Is it true, as some allege, that the headquarters of the Taliban is in or around the Pakistani city of Quetta?" And General Jones responded, "That is generally accepted. Yes, sir." So the Supreme Allied Commander of NATO, which is now in command of the entire military operation in Afghanistan, says the headquarters of the Taliban is in Quetta and yet, the top figures in our administration did not mention this, as I understand it, to President Musharraf when he was here. Rubin Barnett, October 6, 2006, Rubin: Afghanistan at Dangerous Tipping Point.

refrain about growth of Indian influence in Afghanistan, Pakistan's ambitions about hegemony in Afghanistan and keeping line of communications open to Afghan Taliban which could even be useful for the Americans.

Musharraf used the Western fear of jihadis and increasing radicalization in Pakistan to make his regime more relevant to the westerners. Their vulnerabilities were exploited by Musharraf to garner more military and economic aid. After the end of his rule he admitted that the military aid was used in different direction, that is, to shore up security concerns against India.[10]

Even when Gen Kayani took over as COAS and after the installation of civil government it was difficult for the Pak establishment to severe links with the Taliban and jihadi groups. This is despite the fact that Kayani has been considered as one of the secular generals. Maintaining links with the different jihadi organisations, as explained by Arif Jamal in Shadow War: the Untold Story of Jihad in Kashmir does not necessarily depend on having a religious ideology. According to Jamal jihadi organisations were thrilled to hear of the appointment of Gen Kayani as the new chief and many reopened their offices in 2008. Several meetings were said to have taken place between the various Afghan Taliban groups and the Kashmiri jihadis in 2007 by the ISI to help them with a strategy to stop Indian help from reaching Hamid Karzai's government in Kabul and placing more sleeper cells in India for possible activation at later dates. The July 2008 bombings of Indian embassy in Kabul and a repeat bombing by Haqqani group on the instigation of ISI in October 2009 were, in fact, both a warning to India by Pakistan not to meddle in Afghan affairs[11]. Further, the U.S. officials, in July 2008,

---

[10] "Musharraf admits US aid diverted", BBC News, September 14, 2009, available at http://news.bbc.co.uk/2/hi/8254360.stm

confronted Pakistani officials with evidence that Pakistan's Inter-Services Intelligence agency (ISI) is actively helping Afghanistan militants, particularly the Haqqani faction[12]. And these incidents also were evidence of strong linkages between ISI and Afghan jihadi groups.

Mumbai terror attacks were engineered from Pakistan at a time when the democratic government had become more aggressive in asserting its legitimate role in the affairs of the state. Attempting to wrest control of the infamous Pakistan's Inter Service Intelligence Agency (ISI) from the military was one such act that ended in failure. Pakistan military could not let go of an institution which it has used for decades as an in instrument of its internal and external policies arising out of a vision where democratic governments and politicians are considered a threat to security and accommodation with India is an anathema. Further, scenario in Federally Administered Tribal Area (FATA) and adjoining areas of North West Frontier Province (NWFP) where Pakistan military has been fighting an unpopular 'now off and then on' war had been instrumental in creating increased dissonance internally within the Army as well as with the United States on its policies of drone attacks. An additional factor of timing was the forthcoming transition of power in the US and apprehensions of the policies of incoming Obama administration with regard to Pakistan and Afghanistan.

One of the possible goals of Pakistani military-jihadi combine in orchestrating Mumbai attacks was that the post-Mumbai war

[11] "Afghanistan blames Pakistan for Embassy Bombings", October 10, 2009, Reuters report,Afghan ambassador to the United States Said Jawad blamed ISI, "Yes, we do. We are pointing the finger at the Pakistan intelligence agency, based on the evidence on the ground and similar attacks taking place In Afghanistan." Available at http://blogs.reuters.com/pakistan/2009/10/10/afghanistan-blames-pakistan-for-embassy-bombing-india-holds-fire

[12] Mazzetti, Mark and Eric Schmitt. "CIA Outlines Pakistan Links With Militants." *New York Times*, July 30, 2008.

hysteria created by Pakistan military would have enabled it to withdraw from its Western front in FATA and NWFP and deploy forces against India. This was to be and is being used as a bargaining tool against perceived negative policies of the US vis a vis Pakistan. In the event, Pakistani Taliban groups like the Tehrike Taliban Pakistan and many other terrorist groups like Lakshar-e-Toiba volunteered to fight along Pakistani military in case of war against India. That Pakistani military establishment continued to harbour an indulgent attitude towards such groups was clearly visible from the ISI chief, Major General Shuja Pasha's interview to German magazine Der Spiegel in the wake of Mumbai attacks. "*Shouldn't they be allowed to think and say what they please? They believe that jihad is their obligation. Isn't that freedom of opinion*?" He asked, defending extremist rabble-rousers, who have sent more and more Koran school students to Afghanistan to fight in the war there. Such groups have been used as valuable assets and force multipliers by Pakistani military to realise their policy objectives in Afghanistan and India.

US Acceptance of Pakistan's Negative Role

Ideologues and advisers of Obama like Richard Holbrooke had attempted to link solution of Kashmir issue with the Afghan question on the stubborn insistence of Pakistan establishment. Eventually after Obama became President though officially this linkage was abandoned yet the idea that Kashmir has linkage with Afghan issue was not abandoned by Pentagon and State department. Gen McChrystal mentioned about India's rising influence in Afghanistan as a red rag for Pakistan. In a number of Congressional and Senate Foreign Relations Committees' hearings held in 2009, US Central Command Commander General David Petraeus, General Stanley McChrystal, US Commander in Afghanistan and US Ambassador to Afghanistan retired Lieutenant General Karl Eikenberry came out as apologists for Pakistan when specifically asked about 'dual-track' policy of Afghanistan regarding Pakistan Taliban and Afghan Taliban along with many other jihadi factions which have been for long treated as strategic assets by Pakistan.

Petraeus explanation on how Pakistan ultimately takes on the Afghan Taliban and stops funding and promoting this group revolved around U.S. showing more commitment to Pakistan. He told the Senate Foreign Relations Committee *"Frankly, the effort to demonstrate a sustained, substantial commitment to Pakistan — frankly the Kerry-Lugar bill (which provides $1.5 billion) annually in American largesse to Pakistan over five years) is a hugely important manifestation of that — the level of security assistance, foreign military financing, the Pakistan Counter-Insurgency Capability Fund and so forth are also very important, given the history that we have with that country and having left it as you know a couple of times before".* And this was after acknowledging that "the Afghan Taliban are, to be sure, distinct from the Pakistani Taliban and their partner groups, some of which shelter Al Qaeda. They are part of a syndicate of extremist groups that includes both Laskhar-e-Tayiba — the group that carried out the 26/11 Mumbai attacks — and the Haqqani network, among others."

General Stanley McChrystal, US Commander in Afghanistan, appearing before the Senate Armed Services Committee, praised the Pakistani army saying that "their recent actions over the last year or two against their own internal insurgency are really a good indicator of just how serious they are about conducting counter-insurgency operations and reducing instability on their side." But when asked to reply to questions of Pakistan's dual-track policy he was evasive, in fact, he is said to have effectively filibustered the proceedings as members ran out of allotted time for questions.

Pentagon leadership has been consistently hoping that Pakistan establishment would mend its ways of selective approaches to terrorism. Pakistani explanation of addressing its security concerns by going after only the Pakistani Taliban and not the Afghan Taliban, which it apparently continues to promote for strategic depth against India and as a hedge in case the US decides to cut and run, finds a ready acceptance with Pentagon and State department interlocutors. Condoleezza Rice in the Bush administration was also in favour of preserving a strategic balance in South Asia by giving Pakistan military aid like F-16 jet fighters which was obviously not meant for anti-terror fight.

The new improved Af-Pak strategy announced in first week of December 2009 had a number of hidden agendas. One major issue before the Obama Administration was whether Pakistan will tacitly permit drone and Predator UAV attacks on the core of the Quetta-based Afghan Taliban leadership. Evidently the Pakistani leadership is in no mood to allow these kinds of drone attacks which may yet open another front for them. Though President Obama has been saying that effective partnership with the Pakistani government and military is key element for the defeat of the Afghan insurgency, yet cooperation from Pakistan on tackling Afghan Taliban is absent. Obama and his advisers can only think of "increased attention will be paid to strengthening this partnership through military and economic assistance". But as usual Pakistan will take all the aid it can take, play on the US vulnerabilities and will most unlikely deliver on Afghan Taliban. Audits by the US administration have detailed how billions of dollars have been misused and even fraudulently claimed by the Pakistan military. Throwing good money after bad to recover the investment generally is a trait associated with high-risk takers or in short, gamblers.

London Conference and Beyond: Pakistan's Maneuverings

Developments post Obama's December 2009 version of Af-Pak strategy have been moving in a direction where Pakistan, particularly the Pakistan Army is increasingly becoming a key player in the emerging scenario. While the acronym Af-Pak coined in March 2009 signified the organic link between Afghanistan and Pakistan, it also symbolized that Pakistan was both part of the problem and solution as well; the new revised strategy of December 01, 2009 has laid emphasis on partnership with Pakistan. With the conclusion of a US-Pakistan Strategic Dialogue in March 2010 coming after the London Conference, all the past the U.S. and western remonstrations to Pakistan to do more have been abandoned. In fact, Pakistan has acquired so much self-confidence after its successes against Tehrik-e-Taliban Pakistan (TTP) and London Conference that its Foreign Minister Shah Mehmood Qureshi demanded on the eve of US-Pakistan Strategic Dialogue that the United States should "do more" to help Pakistan since the latter has "already done too much" . Contrast this with Obama sending a letter in end November 2009 through his NSA Gen James Lee Jones to President Zardari to stop providing havens to Al Qaeda and the Taliban and to step up the fight against them[13].

Largely, the central outcome of the London Conference and US-Pakistan Strategic Dialogue has been that Pakistan, (which till yesterday was part of the problem in terms of cross border movement of militants, sanctuaries for insurgent groups and, attacks on NATO logistics supply chain together with less than successful counterinsurgency campaign) was now part of the solution and

---

[13] Karen De young, "Obama Offers new Role for Pakistan", *The Washington Post,* November 30, 2009

responsible to assist the West in the emergence of Afghanistan as a moderate democratic Islamic nation.

Both Gen Kayani and ISI Chief attended the discussions during US-Pakistan Strategic Dialogue and the Istanbul Conference which was precursor to the London Conference signifying acceptance of the relevance and ossified thought processes of Pakistani military establishment in the complex puzzle that Afghanistan is. An indication that America has accepted Pakistan as a power-broker was evident from Richard Holbrooke's statement on a visit to Kabul in mid-February. He opined *"Pakistan's ISI can play a role in negotiations and I support that role. - -Pakistan has an influence in this area and has a legitimate security interest."*[14]

Further in March end, for the first time, Kayani had chaired a meeting of federal secretaries at General Headquarters Rawalpindi to set agenda for the US trip which was a strong reflection as to who is on the driver's seat in Pakistan; the civilian government seems to have been effectively sidelined. The trend of Pakistan military losing its credibility was reversed in post-26/11 scenario and was further consolidated by successes gained in operations against Tehrik-e-Taliban Pakistan in Swat and South Waziristan. Offensive against militants in Bajaur and Orkazai is continuing. But Pakistan Army has refused (as requested by the US) to expand their offensive to North Waziristan[15] where Al Qaeda leadership is headquartered citing shortage of troops and their concerns of Indian threat from at the Eastern borders.

---

[14] Lyse Doucet, "Pakistan's Push for a New role in Afghanistan", BBC News, February 19, 2010, available at http://news.bbc.co.uk/2/mobile/south_asia/8521823.stm

[15] See Rania Abouzed, "Pakistan Military Holds Back in North Waziristan", *Time* magazine, April 17,2010 available at http://www.time.com/time/world/article/0,8599,1982001,00.html

Further, the Pakistan Army has not touched Mullah Omar and its Quetta *Shura,* Hikmetyar and Haqqani groups. (But then even the US has not carried out Drone attacks against Quetta Shura while doing the same in FATA against militants there) The backlash from TTP in the shape of militant attacks on Pakistan government's symbols of power is continuing. Meanwhile General Kiyani has extended Lt. Gen. Shuja Pasha's term at the ISI to enable continuity of ISI's obtuse policies in the region without even informing the civilian government; though he did so after the event. With 18th Amendment to the Constitution, the Pakistan Army Chief's tenure is also likely to be extended by a year to four years[16].

That Pakistan's military considers Afghan Taliban as its strategic assets; they have the ability to manipulate the latter to shape favourable outcome of conflict in Afghanistan too seems to have been acknowledged by the US and allies. From the Indian perspective this is a huge development that will allow Pakistan to shape future discourse in Afghanistan with a regime in Kabul which would be beholden to Pakistan (read Pakistan military) and its world view.

The continuous refrain of Pakistan's military establishment since the days of the Musharraf is that there was a need to make a distinction between a good and bad Taliban and that the Taliban need to be mainstreamed, has been finally accepted. This was also a vindication of Pakistani centrality in conflict resolution in Afghanistan and its role in proposed reconciliation with 'Taliban'. The basic approach formalised at the 60-nations London Conference was cash-for-peace plan aimed at weaning away non-ideological and "moderate" Taliban, fighters with the aim of their eventual participation in the governance of that country. These outfits have

---

[16] For instance see Chinmaya R. Gharekhan, "Pakistan: perceptions, prejudices and politics", *The Hindu*, April 14, 2010

consistently waged war on US & NATO Forces in Afghanistan for the last ten years and are an integral part of Pakistani Army's grand strategy of inducing strategic fatigue among U.S. and NATO and eventually their mission failure in Afghanistan.

The second perspective of the developments is that, having assumed a key role of the arbitrator of the Afghan destiny, Pakistan has already started to flex its muscles. Pakistani Army Chief Gen Kayani, fresh from attending NATO military commanders meeting in Brussels- in end-January- averred that "Pakistan wants a 'peaceful, friendly and stable' Afghanistan; strategic depth isn't about 'controlling' Afghanistan but about ensuring Pakistan doesn't have a long-term security problem on its Western border; India's role in Afghanistan is 'unhelpful'; and more importantly Pakistan wants Afghan state institutions, including the Army and the Police force, to be fashioned in a manner that they don't pose a threat to our strategic interests"[17]. Evidently, it is merely a declaration; unless Pakistan has a certain degree of control over Kabul it can not promote the Kayani doctrine which has been modelled on Zia doctrine with the premise that from Indus to Oxus (Amu Darya) should be the sphere of influence of Pakistan.

The offer by Gen Kayani to train ANA too needs to be seen as an attempt to prevent India usurping any training role for the ANA either at the invitation of the Afghan Government or in collusion with the USA.

The capture of Mullah Baradar the number two in Taliban hierarchy followed by arrests of two shadow Taliban governors from Karachi by the ISI is part of the Pakistan military's drive to demonstrate

---

[17] Zahid Hussain, "Kayani spells out Terms for regional Stability", *The Dawn*, February 02,2010

to the Western Coalition that if the latter wishes to exit they have to depend largely on the former. The arrests also come at an apposite time amid many contradictions and murky goings on engineered by ISI regarding controlling the negotiations with Taliban. Arrests were also timed with the ongoing operations against Taliban stronghold of Marjah in Helmand. Ahmed Rashid, a well-known author on nexus between Taliban and ISI, commenting on the arrests observed that *"Pakistan now wants to dominate any kind of dialogue that takes place."* There were reports that Mullah Baradar was becoming 'too independent' of ISI and was negotiating directly with Karzai government[18]. Further, that ISI still continues to support the insurgents was evident from release of two senior Taliban leaders recently. However, such reports are overlooked by the US administrations by observing that only some parts of the security establishment still support the insurgents.

These developments clearly forecast that Western Coalition working on their immediate interests have allowed Pakistan to shape the future discourse in a manner that does not augur well for strategic stability in the region and may end up in undermining all that has been achieved in the nearly decade long struggle against terrorism. It is hardly important that whether the policy of divide and rule now being attempted by UK and NATO supported by the US will work, what is important from the Indian perspective is that despite

---

[18] For additional analysis see Ashley Tellis, "Beradar, Pakistan, and Afghan Taliban: What Gives", March 2010, Carnegie Policy Outlook brief. Ashley argues that Pakistan's actions do not constitute the "sea change" in its behavior, as some observers have argued. Instead, they represent a recalibration of Pakistan's evolving policy: rather than supporting the declared U.S. goal of defeating the Taliban, the recent arrests exemplify a Pakistani effort to seize control over the process of negotiations and reconciliation that its military leaders believe is both imminent and inevitable in the Afghan conflict. And it is emphatically motivated by the conviction that India, not the Afghan Taliban, is the main enemy to be neutralized in the Afghan endgame.

having excellent relationship with Afghan Government and undertaking significant development projects India has been sidelined.

Likely Future Role: Little or no Change

"Given our assistance to the Taliban and given their conduct, we became alongside the Taliban-ruled Afghanistan a pariah state, barely escaping being put on the list of terrorist states. Peshawar became the city to which the origin of virtually all terrorist incidents in the West were attributed by western intelligence agencies"

- Najmuddin A Shaikh (Pakistani Analyst)[19]

Stubborn insistence of most of the Pakistani interlocutors and policy-makers on including moderate or good Taliban as part of dispensation in Kabul as the only solution to the Afghan imbroglio remains the leit motif of Pakistan's military-security establishment. In their wisdom a Taliban controlled government would be more amenable to their influence or at least the Indian government would have no influence over it.

Pakistan is waiting to claim its self assigned strategic space once the American withdrawal takes place from Afghanistan which according to Pakistan's thought process may take place eventually. Pakistan's leadership has stated many times that a strong prosperous and stable Afghanistan would be in everybody's interest. But then a strong and stable Afghanistan may not be favored by strategic elite of Pakistan. It has not as yet abandoned its visions of gaining illusory strategic depth vis-à-vis India. It was for only six

---

[19] Najmuddin A Shaikh, "Looking Back at our Role in Afghanistan", Daily Times, August 29, 2008 available at http://www.dailytimes.com.pk/default.asp?page= 2008% 5C08% 5C29%5Cstory_29-8-2008_pg32

years of Taliban reign from 1996 to 2001 in Afghanistan that Pakistan had some semblance of so called 'strategic depth'. In a paper written by a think tank in 2003, the Pakistani author even talks of inevitability of an eventual federation between Pakistan and Afghanistan. Historically, a strong and stable Afghanistan has always been a rival of Pakistan and except for Taliban government no other dispensation in Afghanistan has either been under Pakistan's tutelage or favorably disposed to it. A strong government in Kabul has always been a motivator for Pashtun and Balochi nationalism in Pakistan and has raised questions on controversial Durand line, the border between Pakistan and Afghanistan. Pakistan had also entertained vision of extending the strategic depth to include Islamic nations of Central Asia through Taliban held Afghanistan. But Pakistan ended up by exporting fundamentalism, terrorism and instability to Central Asian countries. Therefore, Central Asian countries are as wary as US or India and the rest of international community of a Taliban come back in Afghanistan. However, for its own reasons Pakistan continues to support Taliban and makes a distinction between Taliban and Al Qaeda terrorists. The politically and militarily unstable situation of Afghanistan would enable and encourage Pakistan to continue with its policies in Afghanistan. Pakistan would persist with its agenda of mainstreaming Taliban in Afghanistan so that a 'moderate Taliban' government is installed in power.

In post-9/11 era the then President Musharraf was forced to reverse his policies in Afghanistan at the pain of risking being 'bombed to Stone Age'. Musharraf had then decided on a tactical retreat to protect its strategic assets (nuclear deterrence) and policies in Kashmir. In the current and likely future strategic milieu, Pakistani generals have calculated that the US is no more in a position to issue such dire threats and that the US needs Pakistan military more than they need the US; howsoever wrong they may be in their assumptions. Even now at a time when Pakistan's economic and financial situation is precarious, the USA has more than sufficient leverages to influence Pakistan's negative policies. But the U.S has been willy-nilly accepting Pakistan's negative role in the hope that Pakistan would sooner or later reform itself.

Over reliance of the US on Pakistan's military to bail it out of Afghan quagmire has given shape to the US policies that have yielded hardly any positive results in the past several years of turmoil in Afghanistan. There are many grand bargains and reconciliations waiting to happen in the region before the situation in Afghanistan can be stabilised. What about a bargain with Iran? How about a bargain with Russia and Central Asian countries to remove the vice-like grip of the Pakistani GHQ on the US policies. Alternative routes for logistics for the US and NATO forces can only be realised, and dependence on Pakistan reduced in a meaningful way, if such bargains are made. The emerging Af-Pak strategy continues to wrest heavily on Pakistani support despite the evidence that Pakistan is unlikely to mend its policies in Afghanistan in the near future.

Propping up military and Pakistani state repeatedly, asking India to grant concessions to Pakistan on Kashmir, seeking to preserve balance in South Asia through massive military supplies to Pakistan, accepting Pakistan's negative role in Afghanistan on very weak grounds and asking India to exercise restraint every time a state sponsored terror attack takes place would only whet the appetite of Pakistani military junta for more of the same. The U.S. and its allies in Afghanistan seem to have accepted Pakistan's all encompassing role in Afghanistan at the cost of the other neighbours and regional powers that have legitimate interests in Afghanistan. A substantive regional approach is the only way forward. Even if a moderate Taliban government is established in Kabul it is quite unlikely that it will be a panacea for all the ills of Afghanistan as peace and stability may still remain elusive.

Future Scenarios for Afghanistan and Policy Options for India

Background

Predicting the future is always a hazardous exercise. However by evaluating the past and current trends and considering the impact of multiple drivers of the situation it may be possible to develop reasonably realistic alternative scenarios. Scenario building is one of the major tools of the practice of net assessment first brought into vogue by the Office of Net Assessment in Pentagon. Structured process of policy making, as is being increasingly accepted, begins by writing scenarios[20]. Scenarios are plausible views of alternative futures and their impact on country's politico-security environment and can be used as tools to fashion national security strategies in an uncertain, dynamic and challenging environment. The deteriorating security situation in Afghanistan has become a cause of concern for its neighbours in particular and the international community in general. An assessment of possible scenarios for which India needs to develop various policy options as these would have major implications for India and the international community.

Events in Afghanistan seem to be turning a full circle; the security situation in Afghanistan could be said to be fast moving towards a scenario which may resemble what was obtaining just before September 2001. The new US administration under the

---

[20] For instance see Raja Menon and Rajiv Kumar, "Get That Vision 2014", The *Times of India*, April 14, 2010; Admiral Raja Menon (retired) is former Chairman of Task Force on Net Assessment of the NSC and Rajiv Kumar is Director of ICRIER.

leadership of President Obama announced its strategy to deal with Afghan situation in March 2009 which was followed by a review in December 2009. Further, at London Conference in end January 2010, a script was laid out on the ways and means to deal afresh with the rising crisis in Afghanistan. After fresh reinforcements Operation *Moshtarek* was launched against the entrenched Taliban in Marjah in Helmand province in mid-February which is said to have met with some degree of success. Preparations for Operation *Omid* against Taliban strongholds in Kandahar have been under way since then and it was expected to commence in June.

Rising violence and all time high fatalities among the US and NATO troops and Afghan civilian causalities are exerting pressure on the domestic public opinion in troop contributing countries leading to calls for putting into effect an exit- strategy. There is, therefore, dwindling support among the ISAF contributors to provide more troops even as they scrape the bottom of the barrel for other resources. The collapse of the Netherlands government on the question of extending the mandate of its troops in Afghanistan highlights the difficulties which troop contributing nations face at the domestic political level[21]. While the security situation shows no sign of improving in the near term the political situation in Afghanistan also remains tenuous. Equation between President Karzai and the American leadership and western allies had become tense due to Karzai's assertions of interference by the West with the aim of weakening him[22]. Karzai believes that Washington wants regime change in Kabul and that the corruption issue is being used to

---

21 Nicholas Koulish, "Dutch Government collapses over its Stance in troops for Afghanistan",*The New York Times*, February 21, 2010

22 "More Nasty Surprises to Come from Afghanistan", *Speigel online,* April 6, 2010 available at http://www.spiegel.de/international/world/0,1518,687418,00.html

delegitimise the current government. However, of late, after Karzai's visit to Washington in May 2010 some of the irritations that had crept in the relationship seem to have been removed.

Further problems of governance, lack of development, rampant corruption and mismanagement of aid funds are adding to the woes of the common people. Lofty goals as spelled out in Afghanistan National Development Strategy and Millennium Development Goals grandly announced after elections in 2005 and London Conference of 2006 have made little or no progress; benchmarks and timelines laid out in most of the cases have been missed. What is more, lack of any alternative means of livelihood has given incentives to the impoverished Afghans, especially in Helmand and some of the other provinces where Taliban is dominant to grow ever increasing amounts of opium. Taliban, adept in perception management, has very deftly exploited the weaknesses of the present Afghan dispensation to enlarge its area of influence in Afghanistan. In addition revenues from drug-trafficking and other illegal sources have helped Taliban to sustain and maintain its cadres with arms supplies, equipment and other logistics. There are also reports suggesting that contributions from the Gulf countries and Saudi Arabia account for larger proportion of Taliban resources than its pickings from the drug trade.

While Taliban has been gaining ascendancy the security sector reforms for strengthening Afghan National Army (ANA) and Afghan National Police (ANP) are still in their infancy. Both forces suffer from a number of inadequacies in recruitment, training, equipment, attraction and retention. Cases of Taliban sympathizers infiltrating the Afghan security forces are also on the increase adding to the problems of creating a cohesive and strong force to meet the challenges of insurgency and terrorism.

Pakistan and other regional actors have competing interests and political preferences in Afghanistan adding to the Afghan conundrum. While Pakistan remains wedded to the notions of strategic depth and treats Taliban, especially of the Afghan variety, as its asset other regional players are apprehensive of Taliban coming back to power. Yet, mainstreaming of Taliban has become the dominating liet motif of the current US and ISAF nations' discourse. Pakistan is positioning itself as the key power-broker for the future dispensation which may be put in place in Kabul. Another disturbing trend is that the U.S. encouraged by the Pentagon is increasingly seeing the Pakistan army as its strategic and indispensible in rescuing it from the Afghan imbroglio.

With this background this paper will examine the unfolding of American Af-Pak strategy and its dynamics along with the other major situational drivers and gauge into future and arrive at possible scenarios in the near to mid-term and implications of the same from an Indian security perspective.

Critical factors which would drive the alternative future scenarios in Afghanistan are the nature and manner in which the emerging U.S. and Coalition forces' Af-Pak strategy is implemented, internal dynamics of Afghanistan, Pakistan's strategic ambitions and its own internal discourse, role and interests of the regional actors; and capabilities of India in shaping the future environment.

Dominant Drivers of Situation in Afghanistan

Unfolding of U.S. Af-Pak Strategy

The Obama Administration integrated the Bush Administration's ongoing strategy reviews into an overarching 60-day inter-agency strategic review under Bruce Riedel and co-chaired by Ambassador Holbrooke and by Undersecretary of Defense for Policy Michele Flournoy. President Obama announced the new comprehensive strategy on March 27, 2009, accompanied by issue of a "White Paper" of the inter-agency group that performed the review. The strategy announced contained the ends, ways and means to address the 'downward spiral' of overall situation in Afghanistan. Most important was to define the key goals in the obtaining situation; these were outlined as:

(a) Disrupt terrorist networks in Afghanistan and Pakistan to degrade their ability to launch international terrorist attacks;

(b) Promote a more capable, accountable, and effective government in Afghanistan;

(c) Develop self-reliant Afghan security forces that can lead the counter-insurgency with reduced U.S. assistance; and

(d) Involve the international community to actively assist in addressing these objectives.

While the above is only an articulation of the broad policy goals devil lies in, firstly, translating these into definable operational objectives in each of the above areas; secondly, ways and means to achieve them (where definition of success may also be difficult to define); and thirdly, the resources required/allotted for realizing the ends. Despite a number of strategy reviews the U.S. government continues to face decision dilemmas on strategic and operational issues about its engagement in Afghanistan conflict. There is an ongoing debate among the US strategic circles on[23]:-

(a) Defining U.S. national interests in Afghanistan and the region

(b) Defining clear strategic objectives and the desired end end-state based on the those interests

(c) Determining which diplomatic, economic, and military approaches to adopt, and what resources to commit to support approaches

(d) Prioritizing Afghanistan war versus other national security imperatives

(e) Helping marshal a coordinated application of international efforts.

Considered to be an innovative commander due to his performance in his previous appointments General McChrystal (the Commander, International Security Assistance Force and Commander, U.S. Forces Afghanistan till his removal from command in June 2010) in his initial assessment suggested people-centric strategy, that is, to protect the population rather than go out hunting for the Taliban. He also recommended change in procedures to avoid collateral damage especially the civilian causalities. McChrystal opined that there was a possibility of mission failure unless a fully resourced, comprehensive counter-insurgency strategy was pursued. His report given in end August 2009 emphasized the need to reverse Taliban momentum within 12-18 months.

---

[23] Steve Bowman & Catherine Dale, "War in Afghanistan: Strategy, Military Operations and Issues for Congress", CRS Report for Congress, February 25, 2010

One of the most debated aspect of McChrystal recommendations had been a requirement of additional 40, 000 US troops (beyond what Obama's March strategy visualized) as part of the comprehensive 'counter-insurgency' strategy. Though, in a sense this debate has been settled in favour of increased strength approved by Obama on December 1, 2009 yet the manner of fighting the insurgency still remains a debatable point. McChrystal strategy also recommended a major expansion of Afghan forces. On the other hand Joe Bidden, the Vice-President and some others were in favour of a 'counter terrorism' strategy identifying Al Qaeda as the main target to be eliminated which would require much lesser number of troops. Further, sending more troops was expected to reinforce the sense of occupation being felt by Afghans and could become counter productive. Pro-McChrystal advisors had stressed that such number of forces were needed to reverse Taliban ascendancy and create an enabling security environment for the development and roll-out of Afghan governance capabilities. Sacking of McChrystal in last week of June 2010 because of his disparaging comments about civilian leadership may have again opened the debate between adopting counter-insurgency versus counter-terrorism strategy. It is more likely that whatever may be the level of success, post -July 2011 it is more likely that counter terror strategy would be adopted in a phased manner.

There is also question of the definition of success which remains nebulous. Would disrupting and dismantling Al Qaeda in Afghanistan and Pakistan be adequate to address the situation and is it possible to do that without addressing Taliban which has organic links with Al Qaeda? Further, is elimination of Al Qaeda which according to many reports has not been very effective lately, be the only definition of success? A more limited approach which sought a compromise and dilution of resources recommended by McChrystal was more likely to impact negatively the goals of Obama's strategy that also lays stress on improving Afghan government's capabilities for governance and economic development including accelerating the efforts for *Afghanisation* of security forces.

The much awaited review of Obama's initial strategy was announced on December 1, 2009 to an audience of West Point officer Cadets. The new strategy had its three classic components of ends, ways and means to provide a coherent blue print to bridge the gap between realities of today and a desired future as outlined below.

(a) "First, we will pursue a military strategy that will break the Taliban's momentum and increase Afghanistan's capacity over the next 18 months." The 30,000 additional troops were to be deployed deploy in the first part of 2010 – the fastest pace possible – so that eventually they could target the insurgency and secure key population centers. They were also to train additional Afghan Security Forces and improve their counter insurgency capabilities so that eventually they conditions are created for the United States to transfer responsibility to the Afghans.

(b) "Second, we will work with our partners, the UN, and the Afghan people to pursue a more effective civilian strategy, so that the government can take advantage of improved security. This effort must be based on performance. The days of providing a blank check are over." ... "We will support Afghan Ministries, Governors, and local leaders that combat corruption and deliver for the people. We expect those who are ineffective or corrupt to be held accountable. And we will also focus our assistance in areas – such as agriculture – that can make an immediate impact in the lives of the Afghan people."

(c) "Third, we will act with the full recognition that our success in Afghanistan is inextricably linked to our partnership with

Pakistan." ... "*In the past, we too often defined our relationship with Pakistan narrowly. Those days are over. Moving forward, we are committed to a partnership with Pakistan that is built on a foundation of mutual interests, mutual respect, and mutual trust.*"

The components of the new strategy were not very much different from those of the strategy earlier articulated. The overall objective remained the same. The main adversary has been identified as Al Qaeda and not Taliban; therefore this formulation has been questioned by many. It is Taliban which has been causing more harm to the coalition troops than Al Qaeda per se. However, reversing Taliban momentum is also one of the goals articulated in the US strategy.

While the earlier strategy had not talked about an exit date or exit plans the December strategy talked about deadlines for reduction of troops/ withdrawal of troops. There was also allotment of additional means in terms of troops and other resources under the new strategy. Strengthening and building capacities of Afghan National Army and Afghan National Police, civilian surge, looking for reconciliation with amenable Taliban elements, seeking additional contributions from partner countries, involving all the stakeholders and working with Pakistan are the common elements of both the March and December strategies.

Though the March strategy contained no indications for withdrawal of troops (and there was a general understanding amongst the American administration that their presence would be required for at least a decade in Afghanistan) yet Obama did talk about the need for working out an exit strategy. In November 2009 Obama had remarked that "*he wants to finish the job in*

Afghanistan[24]." However, the deadline of 18 months for commencing withdrawal has been criticized on several accounts. Firstly, as far as Taliban are concerned they have to just wait out this period, continue to carry out hit and run attacks without getting involved in pitched battles with the coalition troops and finally claim victory. They have all the time in the world while it is the coalition forces that are looking for an exit strategy. CR Garekhan a former Indian ambassador has remarked incisively that *"The Taliban, for its part, knows that it can win by not losing and the coalition loses by not winning".* Talking about deadlines also does not encourage Taliban to come to the negotiating table.

Further, Pakistan ever the duplicitous ally in war against terror would hardly be persuaded to abstain from extending support to Afghan Taliban knowing that once the Americans and allies cut and run from Afghanistan they would need to do business with Taliban. Secondly, it is also being said that the talk of withdrawal is only meant for domestic consumption where public support for Afghan intervention is fast declining. It needs to be stressed that strategic environment in and around Afghanistan is not conducive for a strategic withdrawal of the US from Afghanistan as the resulting situation could be worse than what is obtaining now. The kind of investments the Americans are making in Bagram and at other places seem to indicate that the Americans would retain their presence in some form or the other even if the drawdown commences on the due date[25]. Thus it is difficult to predict what would be the nature and character of drawdown of forces in circa 2011.

---

24 "Obama Wants to Finish the Job in Afghanistan", BBC News, November 24, 2009 available at http://news.bbc.co.uk/2/hi/8377331.stm

25 "No artificial time table for withdrawal from Afghanistan", *Daily Telegraph*, UK, March 31, 2010; The British Defence Secretary and shadow Defence Secretary are of the view that Gen McChrystal's assessment of 4 to 5 years before the troops can return home is more realistic; but significant drawdown could begin mid-next year. They should return only after completion of their mission.

Trends: Implementing Af-Pak Strategy

The emerging trends in implementation of Af-Pak strategy gained more momentum with the conclusion of London Conference in end January where the broad framework of a 'Compromise and Exit Strategy' seem to have been laid out.

The most dominating objective of the Conference was to evolve strategies to reintegrate the reconcilable elements of the Taliban as part of an exit strategy. On the eve of the Conference, five of the infamous Taliban leaders like the then Foreign Minister of Taliban Government in Afghanistan were removed from the UN Security Council entity list of 144 dangerous terrorists figuring in the sanctions regime under Resolution 1267. And according to some reports the UN representative to Afghanistan, Kai Eide, secretly met Taliban members, ostensibly at militant's request in early January. Secondly, the thrust of conference was also on *Afghanistaion* of the effort and therefore a need to put in effect a transition strategy so that Afghans could take up ownership especially the lead role in the security sector. Thirdly, the focus was on making the Taliban come to the negotiating table through a kind of 'surge and bribe' strategy. And lastly, the need to involve the regional stakeholders was underscored.

While billion of dollars worth of aid was promised during the earlier Conference at London (circa 2006), the latest one focused on providing a cache of $500 million for the reintegration and rehabilitation effort of moderate or so-called 'good Taliban', that is, those elements who could be weaned away from the hard-lined elements or the Taliban leadership through attractive settlement offers. A kitty of USD 140 million has so far been created for Peace and Reintegration Trust Fund to finance the Afghan-led Peace and Reintegration Programme. Moot point is whether after accepting a lucrative offer would the rehabilitated Taliban stay loyal to the Kabul government. There is no way to ensure that they would not go back to their erstwhile masters after availing of the largesse.

Talking to Taliban seems to have acquired an increased urgency in case the timeline of drawdown have to be strictly adhered to because of the political, financial and strategic imperatives of a prolonged war. Pakistan and the notorious ISI along with Saudi Arabia with their pre-dominant Wahabi-Sunni proclivities remain the preferred instruments of talking to the Taliban. Pakistan would be suspicious if the Americans or others were to negotiate with Taliban directly without involving Pakistani military security establishment. Many others have been talking to Taliban for sometime. According to Ahmed Rashid a well known expert on Taliban, one such meeting with Taliban leaders took place on January 8 in Dubai. He has stated in a guest column of BBC that

"According to my last count and information, diplomats or intelligence agents from Britain, Norway and Germany as well as several humanitarian agencies such as the United Nations and the International Committee of the Red Cross have met with Taliban officials either in Pakistan or Afghanistan over the past 12 months,"

Thus London Conference only gives a kind of ex-post facto sanction to the efforts that have been underway for talking to Taliban much before the articulation of Obama's strategy. On the other hand the discourse among the American also seems to be divided. The US Director of National Intelligence (DNI), Admiral Dennis Blair in a testimony to the Senate Committee on Intelligence testified that *"we are losing ground to the Taliban and insurgents in Afghanistan who are now virtually indistinguishable from al Qaeda. These terrorists who have long found sanctuary in the border area between Afghanistan and Pakistan not only directly threaten U.S. national security, they threaten our allies by insisting on spreading their violent and distorted interpretation of Islam. So as we balance forces from Iraq to Afghanistan, how will we protect the gains in Iraq while stopping the slide in Afghanistan?"* In another official document Quadrennial Defence Review released in early February 2010, construct of Taliban as the enemy is missing. It says "Along with our allies and partners, we have renewed efforts to help the governments of Afghanistan and Pakistan disrupt, dismantle, and defeat Al Qaeda and eliminate its safe havens within both nations". That the American officialdom speaks in many different voices is well known and this tendency does not inspire much confidence in their motives and articulated strategies.

Strengthening the Afghan National Security Forces

Further, the goal of *Afghanisation* of the security effort in a short time frame appears to be very ambitious. The final communiqué from the summit in London stated that it welcomed Afghanistan's goal of taking charge of the *"majority of operations in the insecure areas of Afghanistan within three years and taking responsibility for physical security within five years"*. When 100,000 US/NATO/ISAF troops or so equipped with most modern weaponry and equipment have not been able to bring peace and stability to Afghanistan, how can a force planned to be raised to 171,600 by October 2011 which is less sophisticated and less robustly trained and without adequate cohesion and esprit de corps can achieve something better than their mentors?

However, strengthening of both Afghan National Army and Afghan National Police is one of the critical pillars of Obama's strategy. It is widely accepted that unless the ANSF take on the responsibility of security it may not be possible for the international community to disengage from Afghanistan. The draw down of the

American and other forces can only begin in July 2011 once the planned capability development of ANSF has been achieved up to the required degree in order to take the lead role. The process of strengthening the ANSF commenced by the previous US administration six years ago has not made much headway due to many contextual problems. The western analysts and many official documents have reflected upon the mixed results of the efforts so far made in the areas of manning, training, funding, equipping and motivating the ANSF.

Even the assessment of numbers of personnel required has been continuously changing due to resurgence of Taliban. According to the latest requirement the ultimate size of the ANA and ANP (by the year 2013) though still subject to Congressional approval has been pegged at 240,000 ANA troops and 160,000 ANP by the year 2013. Evidently there would be problems of recruitment, attraction and retention. The table and graph below depicts the timelines for shoring up the strength of ANSF.

ANSF Development Goals

ANSF Strength	November-2009 Actual	Oct 2010 Goal	Oct 2011 Goal	Aspiration for 2013-2014
ANA	97, 011	134,000	171,600	240,000
ANP	93,809	109,000	134,000	160,000
Total ANSF	190,820	243,000	305,600	400,000

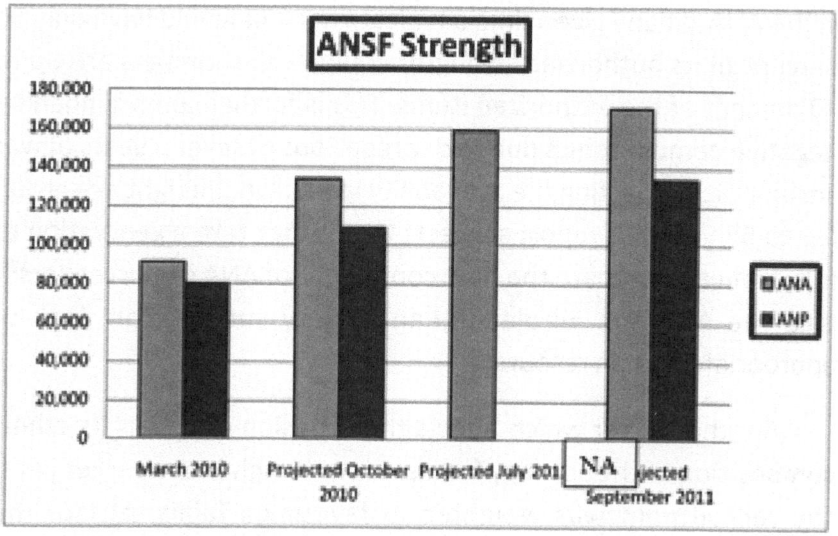

Source: Adopted from DoD FY 2011 Budget Request. February 2010. Pg. 40.

(Tentative projections for ANP by 2013 not depicted in above graph)

Raising such a large force in the given timelines is a daunting task. This is further compounded by a mixed potpourri of several NATO and ISAF nations mentoring and training the ANA and ANP which add to the problems of imparting a standard training and imbuing a common ethos in the ANA and ANP. Problems are also due to cultural differences between the trainers and trained; desertions due to lack of motivation and inadequate compensation. Thrust of training of ANA is also more on training them in either constabulary duties or on rear area security duties rather than making ANA into a regular standing Army that can look after both internal and external security. There is also a shortfall of over 50 percent in the assessed number of trainers required for training ANSF.

Many of the US military reports speak of poor leadership standards of the ANSF. The desertion rates are 20 percent and above in the ANA. At any given time a typical ANA unit would have only 50 percent of its authorized strength; equipment shortages are up to 40 percent of the authorized items. This is further compounded by negative demographics due to depredations of several years of war and conflict impacting the availability leaders in the right age group (35 to 55 years). A report suggests that it may take a generation to fully train and prepare the next contingent of ANA senior leaders[26]. Like the ANA the whole Afghan society suffers from lack of appropriate human resource.

Another factor which affects the cohesion of ANA is its ethnic composition of the security forces. Even though in the earlier years the recruitment was weighted in favour of Tajiks, of late the composition reflects generally the ethnic mix of all the major ethnicities. According to a DOD Report of April 2010 the force is roughly in line with broad demographics of the country, that is, about 41% Pashtuns, 34% Tajiks, 12% Hazaras, and 8% Uzbeks. However, those Pashtuns who are in the force are disproportionately eastern Pashtuns (from the Ghilzai tribal confederations) rather than southern Pashtuns (mostly Durrani tribal confederations). Largely the officer cadre is of Tajik ethnic origin; the graph below depicts the ethnic composition along with the percentages of officers, NCOs and enlisted men. This creates its own dynamics and ethnic tensions.

---

[26] Steve Bowman and Catherine Dale, "War in Afghanistan; Strategy, Military Operations, and Issues for Congress", Congressional Research Service Report, February 25, 2010, p.40

Ethnic Composition of ANA Personnel Compared with Ethnic Mix of the Population

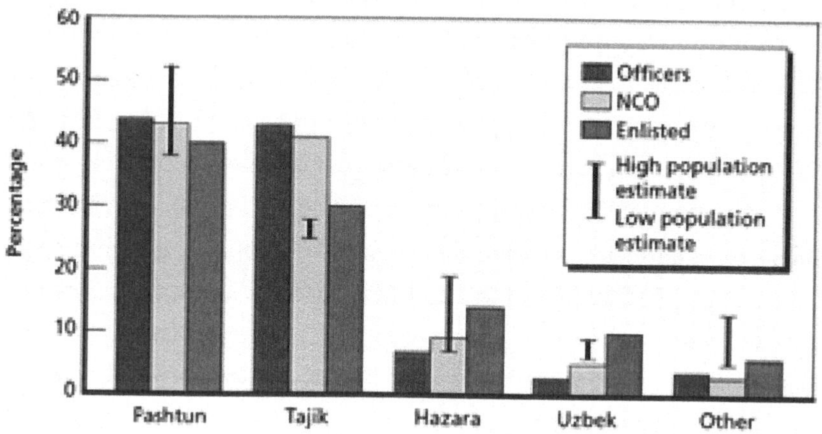

Source: Younossi, Obaid et al. "The Long March Building an Afghan National Army." *RAND*. 2009. Pg. 22

There are over about 100 ANA battalions or *Kandaks* as they are called; they have embedded Operational Mentoring Liaison Teams from the US and NATO countries to guide and provide them with something like on the job training. Overall objective is to enhance the effectiveness of ANA units. According to American analysts the emphasis has been on quantity rather than quality of the units being created to meet the timelines. And the force development goals have been set so high that they are unlikely to be achieved; also there is a tendency to submit false progress report cards. Problems in pay, promotion, corruption, inadequate facilities and equipment, poor medical care, overstretching or over committing force elements, problems in supporting families, vulnerability to Taliban infiltration and threats, and a lack of meaningful compensation for death and disability have been identified as areas which have to be addressed to make ANA a viable force.

The problems of ANP are more acute than that of ANA; it has been recognized that it substantially lags the ANA in its development. Corruption is rampant and the common people lack confidence in ANP. The desertion rates are said to be higher than those of ANP. There are reports to suggest that as much as 78 percent of ANP personnel have not received meaningful training in policing duties. The other negative characteristics of the force are prevalence of substantial illiteracy; involvement in local factional or ethnic disputes because the ANP works in the communities its personnel come from and wide spread use of drugs. (April DOD Report). They are tied to local politics and power brokers and thus are less effective and are unable to win popular support. ANP suffers from chronic shortages of equipment, lack of ammunition and vehicles. There have been cases of ANP officers selling vehicles and equipment and misappropriating the proceeds.

Colossal amount of money ($11.47 billion for ANA and 6 billion for ANP up till December 2009), at least by South Asian standards, has already been spent on development of ANSF without commensurate results becoming visible on the ground. Request to the U.S. Congress for the Financial Year 2011 includes another 11.6 billion dollars for development of ANSF. Instead of US and the western countries training and equipping ANSF it may be more economical to outsource some of these activities to South Asian countries like India and others.

On another level, the Pakistan Army Chief also had reservations about increasing the strength of ANA to such a level that might be of concern to the Pakistan army. General Kayani in early February, 2010 after the London Conference stated that "it would be a cause of worry for Pakistan if Afghanistan's projected army developed the potential to take on Pakistan". It also needs to be remembered that a larger Soviet Russian force supported by the then ANA, though under somewhat different circumstances, had to withdraw. Sanctuaries and training camps on the eastern side of Durand Line has been a common feature in situations obtaining then and now.

As discussed above strengthening of Afghan National Army and Afghan National Police, equipping and training them in 18 months to undertake independent operations on their own does not appear to be feasible.

However, in the Operation *Omid* against Taliban strongholds in Kandahar which is expected to commence in the middle of this year (and wind up by August) the phrase of 'mentoring' the ANA is being replaced by the concept of 'partnering'[27]. According to Admiral Mike Mullen the Chairman, Joint Chiefs of Staff, in this operation the Afghan forces would take the lead role and it would also be different in many ways from Operation Moshtarek executed against Taliban in Marjah. Though the military objectives of Operation Moshtarek seem to have been met by end March it would take another six months to judge the overall success in wresting the control of the area from the Taliban. In fact, the operations in Marjah seem to have been only partially successful and this has been recognised by the U.S. leadership[28]. Further, President Karzai has declared that there would be no attack on Kandahar without the permission of the local

---

[27] John D Mchugh, "On the Frontline with Afghanistan's Army", *Channel 4 News*, April 01, 2010 at http://www.channel4.com/news/articles/world/asia_pacific/on+the+ frontline+with+afghanistanaposs+army/3598157

[28] For instance see Congressional Research Service Report by Kenneth Katzman,"Afghanistan: Post Taliban Governance, Security and U.S. Policy" dated May 11, 2010

tribal elders[29] (at a gathering in Kandahar city where Gen. McChrystal was also present). As part of the strategy of *'shape, clear, hold and build'* the ISAF, ANA/ANP will remain to provide security for the population, the government administration and those undertaking reconstruction activities. How long will the coalition forces hold remains uncertain given the increased propensity on the part of many ISAF nations to make a quick exit?

Success in Kandahar could turn the tide and enable the western forces to break the momentum of Taliban. However, Obama's new strategy remains critically dependent upon the capability development of ANSF and transfer of the lead role to ANA; before then it will be well nigh dangerous to draw down by mid-2011 or cut and run thereafter. Some estimates assess that the ANSF capability development will require time up to 2014-15 before it can be handed over independent operations.

Democracy and Governance

Tensions between President Karzai and the US and other western nations had been building up since he was elected President last year amongst allegations of vote-rigging. Repeated criticism by the US and western leadership of violation of democratic practices by Karzai, being lax in disregarding the corruption and narcotics trafficking charges against his relatives and warlords and asking him to do more 'to clean up his act' has put pressure on Karzai to react in ways that are unpalatable to the west. He had gone to the extent of rhetorically threatening to join forces with the Taliban. Further, Obama has not given the protagonists in the Afghan war the certainty that he is in it for the long haul; the Afghan factions (including regional stakeholders like Iran and Pakistan) have judged

29 Christopher Bodeen "Karzai to Consult Tribes before Offensive", *The Washington Times*, April 05, 2010

that the American interest in Afghanistan is waning and it is the right time to make their own equations in a post-U.S. scenario. Karzai's pronouncements are also a reflection on the diminished authority of the Obama administration and its standing in Afghanistan and the region[30]. However, political tensions seem to have eased up after Karzai's meeting with Obama in May.

One thing which stands out clearly is that corruption is not a phenomenon which is exclusive to the present Afghan dispensation. The American and western contractors in both Afghanistan and Iraq have been in this game for long and have more access to funds than the impoverish government of Afghanistan. Most of the aid for development purposes does not go through the Afghan government and large portion of it is phantom aid. After receiving billion of dollars meant for training Afghan National Police in the last eight years, the US-firm of Dyncorps contracted to train is the subject of several investigations by the U.S. government.

Evidently, there is no alternative to a coordinated politico-military-diplomatic approach in tackling the larger problem of rising Taliban insurgency. The military strategy can not be out of sync from the bigger political strategy. Further, any kind of political tensions are likely to serve the cause of Taliban more than the objectives laid out in Obama's Af-Pak strategy. Karzai has also taken steps to cozy up to Iran, Pakistan and China and even with the Taliban so as not to remain on the wrong side of the power equation that may emerge after the expected withdrawal of the U.S. and its allies.

At the domestic level Karzai held a Peace Jirga in first week of June for obtaining broad support behind the emerging policy. Afghan

---

[30] For instance see Foud Azmi, " Afghanistan and Decline of American Power", *The Wall Street Journal*, April 09, 2010

consultative peace jirga earlier proposed by Hamid Karzai to be held in May this year was postponed on the behest of US elite dictating the dominant narrative on Afghanistan because of their political differences with Karzai. It was only after Karzai's visit to the US during May and discussions with Obama that the US leadership gave a go ahead for Karzai's efforts in reintegrating Taliban. Karzai's peace jirga, in fact, rhymes well with the oft-stated goal of Obama's Af-Pak strategy of '*Afghanisation* of effort'. Further, there was also a possibility of an adverse impact on the forthcoming operation *Omid* against Taliban in Kandahar if Karzai was not brought on board. Earlier Operation Masharak in Marjah has only been a partial success. A greater degree of success in Kandahar would be crucial if ascendancy over Taliban is to be established and the insurgents are forced to come on the negotiating table.

Further, even though it was a large gathering yet some of the key members of the opposition gave the peace jirga a miss alleging that the whole process was orchestrated by Hamid Karzai and he had selected the members of the jirga. Also many others had questioned the efficacy of such a large gathering to come to some kind of consensus. There were others who see no positive outcome of from the meeting as many such jirgas have taken place earlier without much being realized on the ground.

However, eventually 28 consultative committees were formed to arrive at a modicum of understanding on the issues before them. Apparently the committees did reach a decision and finally a resolution of 16 articles was adopted. Main themes continued to be a call to Taliban and groups like Hizbe Islami of Hekmatyar to avail of the 'rare opportunity' to join the process. Karzai has offered to de-list the top Taliban leadership from the UN entity list and has suggested Turkey or Saudi Arabia as countries where talks with Taliban could be held. The resolutions included appeal for stopping night raids by foreign forces and asked President Karzai to clean up corruption.

Another resolution called for the release of Taliban prisoners and suggested that women be sent to meet Taliban wives and mothers to press on them the need for peace. The head of the jirga and former president Burhahuddin Rabbani also appealed the insurgents to renounce violence. To indicate that he was a man of action Karzai and was committed to the resolutions of the jirga he has constituted a committee that will look into all files of arrested Taliban for the purpose of releasing those who do not face any charges.

As for as Taliban are concerned their response has been very negative saying that jirga was aimed at hoodwinking the Afghan people. Taliban has rejected consultative peace jirga's demand that they should lay down weapons and join the peace process; instead they have vowed to continue their resistance till the withdrawal of foreign forces from Afghanistan. The Taliban foot soldiers attacked the Jirga gathering on the first day but fortunately there were no causalities. ISI and Pakistani security establishment would also not be very happy if they were kept out from the negotiating table[31]. Any process which does not enable the ISI to manipulate the emerging discourse in favour of their notions of strategic depth would be opposed and dealt with.

Largely, the peace jirga seems to have endorsed Karzai's leadership of the troubled nation and especially at a time when his credibility was at a low level after corruption complaints and last year's election fraud allegations. He has been able to re-establish his credentials and relevance to the Afghan peace process before

---

[31] For a detailed analysis see M.K. Bhadrakumar, "Hamid Karzai's reconciliation Strategy",*The Hindu* , April 16, 2016

the international community especially the western donor nations. This would also be useful to Karzai's standing when the next international conference on Afghanistan takes place in Kabul in July and he requests for more funds and commitment on long and sustainable basis from the international community. Yet the consultative jirga is hardly a panacea for dealing with the all the ills which afflict a nation that has seen continuous turmoil for last three decades. For the regional and international community any step which brings peace and stability to Afghanistan and prevents extremist and fundamentalist forces taking over Afghanistan would indeed be welcome.

Definitely, governance in Afghanistan is another factor which has not inspired much confidence in the international community and especially in the ability of the current regime in Afghanistan. Will governance improve in the next 18 months or so that international community starts withdrawing? This does not appear likely. Though civil surge is part of the Obama's strategy the international community needs to invest and ensure a sustained commitment to Afghanistan otherwise the situation is more likely to unravel sooner than later creating enhanced challenges and threats to region in particular and international community in general.

Taliban's Ascendancy

The Taliban resurgence cannot be said to have come about just out of the blue. The U.S.'s neglect of the Afghan theatre after its involvement in the Iraq War of 2003 and Pakistan's security establishment's duplicitous policies have been the two basic reasons for the Taliban renaissance. The Taliban's graph of success commenced rising in mid-2006 which started attracting additional NATO/ISAF forces. The security situation has continued to drift since then with ever increasing fatalities of the coalition troops and loss of influence by the Karzai government. A number of reports have indicated that Taliban has influence in 70 to 80 percent areas of Afghanistan. Taliban has gained ascendancy particularly in areas where Pashtuns are dominant[32]. (See the graphic below)

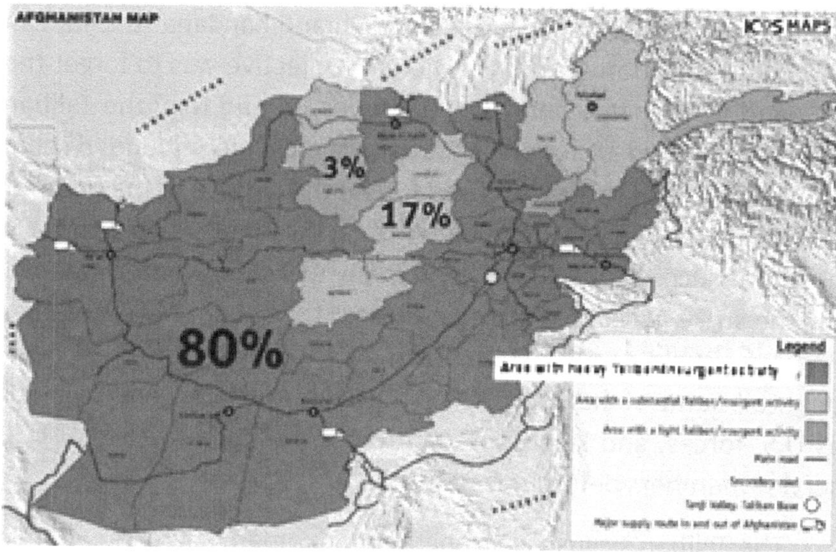

Taliban/Insurgent Activity

Attacks throughout Afghanistan in the shape of suicide bombing, IED blasts and even direct attacks continued unabated throughout 2009 and the momentum is being maintained in the current year. The US troops by end December 2009 (316) were twice the level of 2008 (155); and they have already crossed one third of the last year in early April 2010[33]. By early June the overall American casualties in Afghanistan had crossed the figure of 1000 and the battle has been getting deadlier since then. Even though some success has

---

32 See The International Council on Security and Development (formerly Senlis Council) report "Struggle for Kabul: The Taliban advance", December 2008

33 i.Causalities.org Operation Enduring Freedom http://icasualties.org/oef/

been achieved in Marjah it is not yet clear that it is a permanent success and not transient. Impending operations in Kandahar are likely to see more intense battle with more potential for loss of human lives. The year 2010 may turn out to be the deadliest year if the current trends continue.

As a riposte to operations in Marjah and Kandahar the Taliban launched operation *Al Fateh* or victory. Objective was to target the U.S. and NATO bases and isolated troops. In end May the Taliban carried out a bold attack on Kandahar airfield which wounded some NATO troops and contractors and forced the closure of the base for several hours. Though, the Taliban attack cannot be said to have been not successful as it suffered many casualties during the raid yet the strike gave a psychological boost to Taliban. A week earlier Bagram airfield north of Kabul, the main coalition base had been targeted. Some of the insurgents in the Bagram attack were disguised as U.S. forces, and killed one contractor and injured several U.S. service members before retreating[34].

The Taliban's cause is strengthened by many factors; endemic corruption, weak governance, profits from narco-trafficking which are used to fuel the insurgency, sanctuaries for training and other support across the Durand Line and successful perception management operations. Further, according to a Congressional Report of June 2010 protection payments for safe passage of logistics and supplies for American and NATO troops are a significant potential source for funding of the Taliban[35]. Thus with multiple sources of generating funds the Taliban is also able to pay attractive salaries

---

34 Alan Cullison and Maria Abi-Habib "Afghan Raids Show Taliban will persist among losses", Wall Street Journal, Asia edition, May 24, 2010

35 Report by Rep. John F. Tierney and staff, "Warlord Inc., Extortion and Corruption along the U.S. Supply Chain in Afghanistan" June 2010 available at http://www.cbsnews.com/htdocs/pdf/HNT_Report.pdf?tag=contentMain;contentBody

to its foot soldiers to the tune of US dollars 200 to 300 per month which are better than what is being paid to ANA and ANP personnel.

Many studies and reports originating in the West have stressed on the umbilical cords between the ISI and the Taliban, Jalaludin Haqqani and Gulbodin Hikmetyar groups[36]. A London School of Economics report of June 2010 outlines the involvement of ISI in terms of guiding the Taliban in strategy and operations, providing sanctuary and funding, supplies and ammunition; and training and recruitment. Some of the skills and capabilities exhibited by the Taliban insurgents at the operational and tactical level suggest the involvement of trained military personnel[37].

Further the lack of coordination between the various NATO/ ISAF nations handicapped by their national caveats also helps the Taliban indirectly. The large number of civilian causalities resulting from so-called collateral damage either through air attacks or through other kinds of kinetic operations has created a rising tide of anger against the coalition forces. Civil casualties have been increasing year on year which helps Taliban win more recruits for their cause.

The effects of billion of dollars worth of aid promised to Afghans to support the Afghan National Development Strategy are not visible on the ground. Most of the developmental aid does not even reach Afghanistan and mostly it is not routed through the Afghan government. Many reports have indicated that the extent of the phantom aid is over 80 percent[38].

---

[36] For instance see Alan Kronstadt, "Pakistan-US Relations" U.S. Congressional research report, February 2009.

[37] Matt Waldman, "The Sun in the sky: the Relationship between Pakistan's ISI and afghan Insurgents", discussion Paper No. 18, Crisis States Research Centre, Development Studies Institute, LSE, June 2010

[38] Matthew J. Nasuti, "America's Phantom aid to Afghanistan:", *Kabul Express*, October 23, 2009 avaialable at http://kabulpress.org/my/spip.php?article4211

The Taliban that has emerged at present is more robust, better trained and more battle experienced especially against the tactics of the western troops. They are savvier and have shown that they are capable of strategic planning and coordinated action. They have exploited the grievances of the local population and thus have gained sway over Pashtun dominated areas.

Implicit in the above is that unless the Taliban are denied its launch bases and local support -through a sustained application of military power, area domination and delivery of god governance and justice the US and ISAF are unlikely to reverse the Taliban's momentum. By bringing in Pakistan's military and ISI as a preferred partner to solve the complex issue of Afghanistan is hardly likely to serve the goals of the US Strategy.

Pakistan: Jostling for Primacy

As discussed at length in the section on Pakistan's interference in Afghanistan, Pakistan has been able to obtain substantial endorsement from the U.S. and coalition partners of its approach. Post London Conference Pakistan military's and ISI links with the Taliban are being viewed somewhat as necessary to solve the Afghan puzzle. That Pakistan's military establishment along with the ISI has been attempting to become key arbitrators of Afghanistan's destiny has been brought out in the previous section of this paper. Further, as revealed by a number of Western reports and especially the London School of Economics report of June 2010 that Pakistan ISI is intimately involved in supporting the activities of the Taliban to the extent that it has representatives on the Quetta *shura* and the Haqqani command council. The ISI, according to the report, has circumscribed the Taliban's strategic autonomy, precluding steps towards talks with the Afghan government through selective arrests of some of the Taliban leaders. While commenting on London School of Economics report General Petraeus remarked that "you have to have contact with bad guys to get intelligence on bad guys". But then this has not been the only report or study which have highlighted the Pakistan security establishment's links with the Taliban and other insurgent groups.

A Rand report of June 2010 on Pakistan's approach to counter insurgency[39] concludes that Pakistan's record against the militants remains a mixed bag, with the country lacking a comprehensive counter-insurgency doctrine and the militants continuing to be a significant threat to Pakistan, the region and the world at large. Besides finding fault with its counter insurgency campaign in FATA and affected areas of NWFP (now Khyber Pakhtunkhwa) the report recommends, "Pakistan needs to abandon militancy as a tool for its foreign and domestic policy. A key objective of US policy must be to alter Pakistan's strategic calculus and end its support to militant groups. The US should continue to make this position clear, as it began to do in 2010". The report also cautions the U.S. to reduce it reliance on Pakistan where feasible. And most importantly the Report advises that "the US should re-examine 'carrots' and 'sticks' in a comprehensive strategy. The US should continue US Special Operations Forces training programmes and ensure that goods and services given to Pakistan are appropriate for counter-insurgency purposes. But it should withhold some aid until Pakistan makes discernible progress. Washington has had mixed success in persuading Pakistan to change course, partly because US strategy has focused too much on carrots and too little on sticks."

Despite many such studies and reports, Pakistan has been rarely confronted with such evidence, especially by the Pentagon. Looking

---

[39] Seth G. Jones and Christina Fair, "Counter Insurgency in Pakistan", Rand Report of June 2010 available at www.**rand**.org/pubs/monographs/2010/**RAND**_MG982.pdf

at the emerging trends even President Karzai is now more inclined to negotiate with Pakistan. Reports emerging in end June indicate that Pakistan's security establishment had arranged a meeting of Sirajudin Haqqani (son of Jalaludin Haqqani) with President Karzai for talks on power sharing arrangements.

Involving Regional Players

Emerging trends indicate that despite declarations about involving regional stakeholders as one of the main planks of Af-Pak strategy, nothing concrete has been done by the US to move towards this goal. Henry Kissinger had also stated last year that the regional stakeholders should do some of the heavy-lifting for security and stability of the region. He also made the point that Afghanistan has powerful neighbours; each is threatened one way or the other and in many respects more than the US is, by the emergence of a base of international terrorism. General Petraeus, earlier the Commander of U.S. Central Command and now entrusted with the direct command of Afghanistan operations after removal of General McChrystal had opined in early January 2009 that "It's not possible to resolve the challenges internal to Afghanistan without addressing the challenges especially in terms of security related to Afghanistan's neighbors. A regional approach is required.... [The Coalition] will have to develop and execute a regional strategy that includes Pakistan, India, the Central Asian States and even China and Russia along with perhaps at some point Iran also[40]". In an article in a magazine he had emphasized again that those seeking to help Afghanistan and Pakistan need to widen the aperture even farther to encompass at least the Central Asian states, India, Iran and even Russia and China[41]. However, the idea of forming a Regional Contact Group has not materialized.

---

40 General David Petraeus, "Remarks," Passing the Baton Conference, Walter E. Washington Convention Center, Washington, D.C., hosted by the United States Institute of Peace, January 8, 2010.

41 General David Petraeus, Interview, *Foreign Policy*, January-February 2009

Additionally Saudi Arabia also needs to be involved because a number of groups and elements in that country support Wahabism and radical Sunni ideology. It was one of the three countries along with Pakistan and UAE that had recognized the Taliban government of Afghanistan. Funds from Saudi Arabian charities and other organisations continue to flow into Afghanistan and Pakistan which find their way to Taliban. Saudi Arabia's motivations are also influenced by the rising influence of Shiite Iran in the region. Saudi Arabia considers that Pakistan's security establishment can help it to reduce the Iranian influence in Afghanistan. President Karzai has, off and on, tried to use Saudi Arabia as an intermediary for talks with Taliban leadership. For reconstruction activities in Afghanistan Saudi Arabia has not contributed much whereas Iran has a major construction programme in Afghanistan especially in the province of Herat.

Cooperation by the U.S. and its coalition partners with Iran remains stymied because of its nuclear ambitions and the American claims that it is following a dual track approach. Even though Iran would not like to see a Taliban Sunni government in place in Kabul, yet it would also like to see an early departure of Americans from Afghanistan because of its own geo-political and geo-strategic interests. There was also a time when the route from Chahbahar port to Afghanistan was under consideration as an alternative logistics supply route for coalition troops but the emerging internal and external dynamics in the region have prevented that option from being exercised. Similarly, there is only a limited cooperation with Russia and Central Asian countries in the form of alternative logistics supply route through Northern Distribution Network which has its own limitations. Attempts by the Shanghai Cooperation Organisation (SCO) with its Afghan Contact Group to improve its salience in Afghanistan are not viewed positively by the US and its NATO allies. They are not in favour of giving SCO any recognition or credibility considering it to be a competing security structure. The toppling of President of Kyrgyzstan in April points to the inherent instability in Central Asian countries bordering Afghanistan. Kyrgyzstan has both Russian and American air bases; for Americans it is the main air base supporting the Afghan effort. Instability in Kyrgyzstan has also created apprehensions in China regarding likely threats emanating from there to the Xingjian region[42].

China is also comfortable in dealing with Afghanistan from a distance even while it is concerned with the likely negative fall out of radicalism and extremism spilling out of Afghanistan and affecting it in Xingjian. On balance it would tend to continue endorsing Pakistan's policies in Afghanistan with an understanding that Pakistan would protect its interests even when the coalition troops pull out. During Karzai's visit to China in March 2010, Beijing chose to focus on increased economic investments and support to Afghanistan and a very limited help in the shape of training Afghan military personnel (about 19 or so) in China[43].

The U.S. would have to involve the regional players in resolution of the Afghan problem by jettisoning its unilateral approach. It could either become a facilitator or the regional approach could be adopted under the aegis of the U.N. However, there are no indications that the U.S. is as yet ready for involving the regional stakeholders. It has made only solemn declarations so far.

Further, the US and its leadership has increasingly become receptive to Pakistan's refrain of reducing the Indian footprint for its

---

42 L.C. Russel Liao, "Implications of Kyrgyzstan revolt on China's Xinjiang Policy", *China Brief*,Volume X, Issue 8, April 16, 2010 http://www.jamestown.org/programs/chinabrief/

43 Richard Weitz, "Karzai's visit highlights Beijing's Afghan Priorities", *China brief*, Volume X, Issue 8, April 16, 2010, Jamestown Foundation available at http://www.jamestown.org/programs/chinabrief/

cooperation with the U.S. as the discussion carried out earlier has pointed out. General McChrystal was one of the fore runners in this field when he pointed out that India's improved signature even though in the developmental field was a cause for Pakistan to take a counter action. Thus he showed an implicit acceptance of Pakistan's right to take offensive actions against Indian interests in Afghanistan even though it is benign and in the interests of the Afghans. Though Gen McChrystal has been sacked his concept on Indian presence in Afghanistan generally resonates among the Pentagon leadership. Therefore, the harsh reality of the matter is that Pakistan is becoming the central player to the exclusion of the regional actors. This trend is unlikely to lead towards a scenario where Afghanistan can be envisioned as a peaceful and stable country in the near to mid-term.

Emerging Scenarios and Alternative Futures

The most important driving factor of the future scenario would be as to how the dynamics of Af-Pak strategy shape up and how it is implemented on the ground. While an ideal strategy could be articulated its implementation on ground would be bedeviled by many factors of friction. There are too many moving parts in the shape of actors with competing interests including allies and adversaries involved that would militate against an ideal execution of the strategy articulated. The gap between articulated and implemented strategy would be the element of friction which would again need to be bridged. Critical uncertainties of emerging strategic scenario would be the degree of success achieved by the US in its goals after defining its Af-Pak strategy objectives clearly and ability of Taliban to sustain the offensive against coalition forces which would in turn be determined by Pakistan's attitude as also Pakistani military success in FATA region.

Long-term commitment of the US to 'invest and endure' rather than looking for an early exit, improved governance, strengthening ANA and ANP, increased engagement of the regional actors, additional contributions by NATO/ISAF/international community, bringing Pakistan in line with the U.S. and its allies goals in Afghanistan rather than allowing Pakistan to shape the discourse and reversing Taliban resurgence would be the key elements of the future scenarios. Further, counter strategy of Taliban and its allies would be another important determinant of evolving future scenario.

In light of the above three simple scenarios can be worked out though additional scenarios depending upon the degree of virulence of the key determinants and a combination of the driving factors and trends could also be worked out. More of the same or status quo, deterioration of situation leading to a calibrated withdrawal and growing stability due to gaining ascendancy over Taliban could be three possible alternative future scenarios of Afghanistan.

Status quo/More of the Same Scenario

Broad contours of this scenario would be relative successes followed by reverses with neither side gaining ascendancy over each other. It is quite evident that as long as the US and NATO led ISAF forces remain in Afghanistan Taliban can not achieve a clear victory. The present period can also be described as a period of strategic stalemate which has a potential to move towards a negative or positive path depending upon the commitment of coalition forces. This scenario is predicated upon limited successes by the US and its partners despite having opted for Counter Insurgency strategy vis-à-vis 'Counter-terrorism' strategy which did not involve much increment in troops and was abandoned. Obama, due to political compulsions and as part of his declared strategy starts drawing down forces from July 2011; in effect returning to counter-terrorism strategy. This is further compounded by political discord between Karzai and the U.S. leadership contributes to the lack of positive outcome of operations against the Taliban strongholds in South and East.

Resolve and commitment of the international forces to persevere in Afghanistan in such a scenario remains weak. There is an incremental enhancement of capabilities Afghan Army and the security forces but their effectiveness remains in question because of tribal loyalties and the problems of forging a cohesive fighting force. Much heralded policy of shifting the focus of 'mentoring' the Afghan forces to 'partnering' with them (that is to give them lead role in operations as part of Afghanisation of the effort) shows mixed results, especially in the major offensive like *Operation Omid* against Taliban in Kandahar.

There could be some improvement on the political front with some moderate elements joining the government due to reconciliation and reintegration efforts. Governance remains Kabul centric while the Taliban writ continues to run in South and East Afghanistan. The government is unable to shape the perceptions of Afghan populace through good governance, development and elimination of corruption thus enabling Taliban to get support from certain sections of the population.

Further, Pakistan army's offensive in FATA and disturbed areas of Pakhtunkhwa meet with a degree of success but Pakistan army is largely ineffective in preventing Taliban's infiltration either through design or default. This would reveal that Pakistan army has gone back to its erstwhile pattern of now-off and then-on mode of operations in FATA and NWFP (now Khyber-Pakhtunkhwa). Thus logistics- lifeline of Taliban remains largely intact and the US cautions Pakistan to do more whereas Pakistan asks for more military and economic aid. The US attempts to activate Afghan contact group to involve regional actors but this step does not move forward because of geopolitical and geo-strategic concerns of the regional stakeholders.

There are two paths this scenario can take from here; one is with further accretion of forces and resources with Pakistan increasingly being nudged in the right direction this scenario moves towards a positive direction leading to reversing of Taliban's ascendancy and growing stability. On the other hand were the gains made during the period to be lost due to confluence of all the negative factors as aforementioned then the scenario could lead to a situation where the US and coalition forces look for declaring some kind of victory and then they make an exit; this scenario has been referred by many as orchestrated or calibrated withdrawal. Alternative could also be that there is a sudden collapse and the foreign forces make a sudden exit instead of a calibrated one.

'Declare Victory and Make an Exit' Scenario

This scenario would be a construct of status quo scenario sliding down hill. This would be due to growing dissonance at both political and military level, inadequacy of troops and inability to execute robust counter insurgency strategy. Fatalities of the US and NATO troops climb sharply especially during Operation Omid and continue to mount raising domestic pressures for withdrawal. Some of the NATO countries like Canada and others refuse to extend the mandate of their troops in Afghanistan. Because of lack of boots on ground the coalition forces would revert to using air power and kinetic means to compensate for limited ground forces. Increased collateral damage would further alienate the population in the arms of Taliban. Despite pouring considerable money and efforts ANA and ANP remains ineffective. All the negative factors of poor governance result in increase of support base of Taliban and little or no progress in national reconciliation or in mainstreaming the moderate factions of militants would be key defining elements of such a scenario. Pakistan continues to play its double game and reverts back to deals with the radicals in FATA and Khyber-Pakhtunkhwa. Coalition forces fail to convince the domestic public opinion about the objective and goals of their engagement in Afghanistan. Regional players stay on the sidelines and are unable to contribute in time to prevent the situation spiraling downwards.

In the face of adverse scenario US congress and people demand immediate withdrawal of US troops. Non-NATO ISAF members gradually start pulling out their contingents, US leaders consider two possible alternatives:

(a) In a final push US launches series of renewed offensive to retake large portions of territory from Taliban, give further onus of ground operations to ANA with US increasingly moving to support role. Above to be followed by political reconciliation with moderate elements within Taliban to join political mainstream through orchestrated loya jirga. Declare 'completion of mission' and pull out majority of forces retaining important bases as advance posts.

(b) Simply cut its losses and withdraw, accepting the negative political and military fallout of mission failure.

Such a situation may also lead towards scenario where Afghanistan plunges into a civil war with many factions/warlords/ other groups getting hold of power in Kabul and then being replaced by a stronger faction with or without the intervention of ISI. Replay of what happened after withdrawal of Soviet Union and then take over by Taliban is a strong possibility.

Taliban Reversed Scenario

Reversing the ascendancy of Taliban leading to growing stability would be the most desired future scenario of Afghanistan. This is premised on breaking the will of Taliban for a sustained resistance. Counter insurgency strategy with increased force levels and a long term commitment of the NATO/ISAF forces along with bringing in the regional players in a meaningful way would be important determinants of this scenario. Pakistan would have to be brought on board increasingly in a positive manner. With its bitter experience in FATA and Khyber-Pakhtunkhwa it sees no benefits in pursuing its notions of strategic depth in Afghanistan (hardly likely). Neutrality of government in Kabul is guaranteed through international covenant.

Additional constituents of this scenario would possibly include, functioning central and regional governments, increase in the capacity of the Afghan National Army and Police to control areas independent of support by international forces. Concomitantly neutralization of support bases of internationally known terrorist groups operating in Af-Pak region such as Al Qaeda, Taliban, Lashkar-e-Taiba would have been successfully carried out or increasingly in progress with effective neutralization or assimilation of these groups in the mainstream. Development of institutions economic, security, governance and civil society will show some progress finally resulting in reduction of external dependence for security, economy and development. This scenario is likely to remain fragile for some time and the gains will need to be consolidated with reintegration of the militants into the mainstream.

Implications and Policy Options for India

The worst case scenario, i.e. the withdrawal of coalition forces has grave implications for the region and international community. The impact of a sudden US strategic reversal and consequent spiraling of violence and Islamic extremism out of Af-Pak region would be mostly felt in India. Islamic radicals would feel reinvigorated and get emboldened to extend their jihad not only to Kashmir but also to India's hinterland. With an air of invincibility after having defeated the erstwhile super power Soviet Union and now the only super power US their ambitions to embark on a global jihad would not hold any bounds. Central Asia, North Caucasus, Europe and other parts of the globe would become their area of operations. Jihadi groups would thus unleash more potent attacks not only in India but elsewhere also.

Pakistan may also have to reap the negative consequences of Taliban-Al Qaeda combine's victory with increasing Talibanisation of FATA and Khyber-Pakhtunkhwa with enhanced threat to security of its nuclear weapons. Taliban would have gained reverse strategic depth in Pakistan and the resulting instability would further threaten India's security. Evidently, return of Taliban in Afghanistan would not be an unmixed blessing for Pakistan as a united Afghan and Pakistan Taliban would pose more challenges to Pakistani establishment.

Training Afghan National Army

So far India has been relying on soft power even though there are some advocates of employing hard power in Afghanistan. Stability in Afghanistan is of vital concern to India. Thus if situation in Afghanistan goes awry would India be willing to consider hard power options? Nevertheless India must ensure good military and political relations with ANA and strengthen it through training and equipment. India has the capability undertaking training programme designed to train anything upto 25 to 30 battalions per year in counter insurgency operations. However, for this India would need to continue to have dialogue with the US and its allies and emphasise the benefits of ANSF being trained by the Indian army which has vast experience in counter insurgency operations and tactics. Training would be much cheaper compared to the exorbitant amounts being spent by the NATO forces for training Afghans[44]. Training would imbibe the ethos of minimum use of force and people friendly activities in contrast to the kinetic operations of the coalition troops. Training will be without any ideological content and in the ambience of shared cultural affinity. To obviate India's role in training ANA General Kayani has offered to train the ANA.

Sending troops would be more of a counter productive option because of the groundswell of backlash it is likely to cause among the proud Pashtuns and other Afghans. Further, there would be the problems of logistics for maintenance of such a force in a country with which we do not share borders. Staging of forces through Iran would also not be easy given the state of our relationship with Iran at the present juncture. Yet, vigorous measures to prevent the type of attacks which have taken place against our embassy in Kabul twice and once against a guest house where Indians were housed need to be taken. Selective targeting of terrorist groups and their leadership is one option which should be considered if our own agencies are up to it.

Establishing strong institutional linkages with ANA which is likely to play a pivotal role in stabilizing the country would serve Indian goals better. Further, even though elements of erstwhile Northern alliance have merged with Karzai's government it would be beneficial to renew links with the components of the alliance as they would hardly be supportive of a Taliban dominated government.

---

44 For instance see Sumit Ganguly, "Let India Train the Afghan Army", *The Wall Street Journal*, February 16, 2010

Expanding India's Engagement

India's investment in development infrastructure has benefited the common people in Afghanistan creating considerable good will among the populace. Historically, India has enjoyed good relationship with Afghan populace. India needs to develop stronger linkages with those political forces in Afghanistan who are opposed to Talibani percepts and concepts. It is believed that large percentage (some estimates indicate 90 %) do not want Taliban to come back. Such groups would include all ethnic communities the Pashtuns, the Tajiks, the Uzbeks and the Hazaras and it is with such groups that India needs to engage further and expand its cooperation. Therefore soft options should continue even while hard options are not taken off the table.

Further, despite the recent set backs due to ISI-inspired attacks on Indian interests in Kabul the Indian efforts in supporting institutions of governance and capacity building need to be re-invigorated; most of the training of Afghan civil officials could be done in India to obviate security concerns. Development assistance and aid could be further enhanced beyond the current levels and third parties involved if enhanced security can not be ensured for the Indian personnel.

Ongoing Indo- US dialogue on developments in Afghanistan and its implications on Indian core strategic interests needs more active engagement with the US; presently the US deferring to Pakistan's sensitivities on the issue refrains from involving India to address the political, military, economic and societal situation in Afghanistan. Convincing the US about India's concerns and sensitivities would be a major diplomatic challenge. Here India must play a pro active role in concert with its interests as a major regional player rather than allow US to shape the discourse.

Dialogue with militants

Opening of dialogue with Afghan militants (some reports indicate that India may have already embarked on this path) particularly those nationalist elements that are concerned with nation building in Afghanistan not so much as Islamic ideology would become imperative. Even a Taliban spokesman has claimed that his organisation did not want India out of Afghanistan but attacked the country for supporting the Hamid Karzai government and western forces. According to him *"If the Taliban return to power, we would like to maintain normal relations with countries including India. It's possible for the Taliban and India to reconcile with each other"*[45]. This is merely a declaration but talking to some of the Taliban groups need not be ruled out. In our own country we have been talking to all kind of insurgent groups off and on.

There are reports of old Northern Alliance constituents who were at one time close to India being behind Karzai's efforts to patch up or reach some kind of accommodation with the Taliban/ Hekmatyar group. From Indian perspective the most important issue is to deny Pakistan a hold on Afghanistan that could not only reinforce its proxy war against India but also fuel Islamic radicalism in the country as discussed earlier. With this being India's principal aim then establishing contact with Taliban groups and establishing leverages which ensure that emerging political discourse does not move towards an Islamic caliphate but a participatory democratic model (suited to Afghan conditions) with all its expected flaws; and that would be in India's interest.

India's remains very cautious about the unfolding reconciliation and integration strategy outlined at London Conference. Our Foreign

---

45 "Taliban say they can reconcile with India", *The Times of India*, March 26, 2010

Secretary remarked in March this year that, "We believe it is imperative for the international community, in its new initiatives on security, reintegration, and reconciliation in Afghanistan, to approach these issues carefully – and with caution. *We believe that any reintegration process should include only those who abjure violence, give up armed struggle and terrorism and are willing to abide by the values of democracy, pluralism and human rights*. There is every risk, otherwise, that the Taliban could resurrect them as they have done in the past even when we think they have been defeated or we are rid of their hardcore elements"[46].

Developing Regional Consensus

India must take a pro active stance in developing regional consensus to build on gains made so far as it has high stakes in Afghan stability. In the emerging discourse India, Russia, Iran and central Asian countries have been increasingly sidelined especially at the London Conference. Common agenda for the region would be the issues of extremism and terrorism, narcotics and its trafficking and trade and transit corridors. Pakistan would have to be brought on board and its security concerns addressed to a degree that does not create security challenges for others. A balance would have to be found between the competing strategic interests of the regional stakeholders for the common good of the region. A friendly and neutral government in Kabul which is bereft of any ideology that promotes jihad would be welcome to all neighbours. A Taliban government in Kabul would hardly be a panacea for all the ills of Afghanistan as peace and stability may still remain elusive. In its strategic dialogue with the US, India needs to continually stress to

---

[46] Address by India's Foreign Secretary Nirupama Rao at Woodrow Wilson Centre on, "Two Democracies: Defining the essence of India-US Partnership", March 15, 2010 available at http://www.wilsoncenter.org/index.cfm?fuseaction=news.item&news_id=605243

the US the need for a regional approach which has been articulated as an objective to be achieved in the Af-Pak strategy; a Pakistan-centric solution is unlikely to bring in long-term stability in Af-Pak belt. Putting all eggs in Pakistani basket is more likely to prove costly for the US and its allies with concomitant negative outcome for Afghanistan's neighbourhood and international community.

China in such a scenario is also likely to be affected party particularly if Pakistan is also reeling under growing radical forces. It would be prudent to initiate regional dialogue perhaps under SCO to forge common strategy to deal with the situation. China is a key player in any future regional coalition seeking to secure and rebuild Afghanistan, particularly after U.S. troops pull out. China reportedly sees revival of Afghan economy as an important parameter for Afghan stability.

Bringing in international forces under the umbrella of the UN would be another viable option but this would not be an easy task given the competing geo-strategic interest of the major players in the region especially of the veto-wielding members of the UN Security Council.

Enhancing Homeland Security Capabilities

Effective steps to protect the country from a backlash of creeping Talibanisation in Pakistan and radicalization of their society are important. Own military and internal capabilities (both paramilitary and police forces) need to be enhanced to meet the challenge of Pakistan military's nexus with the terror groups and new strategies put in place to prevent Mumbai type attacks. As part of pro active stance strikes against terror camps may become inescapable in the developing scenarios even though diplomacy and non-military means would remain a preferred alternative. Some degree of back channel or direct contact with Pakistan must be maintained as also with

China to enhance our leverages. Dismantling of terror infrastructure in Pakistan needs to be continually stressed in all bilateral, regional and international forums.

Conclusion

Unfolding of future scenarios remains largely dependent on US strategies; developments in Pakistan and manner of reconciliation between moderates and radicals would be the other important factors. The Af-Pak strategy has gravitated towards a counter insurgency dominant strategy to achieve success yet the degree of success which the US-NATO combine will achieve remains unpredictable. Laying down of timeline for drawdown of forces has engendered its dynamics with every competitor attempting to claim its own strategic space. Pakistan military establishment is convinced that western forces lack commitment and resolve for a sustained fight and therefore it is waiting to claim its strategic depth in Afghanistan after their eventual withdrawal which could be sooner than later. The US has not involved its coalition partners much in the ongoing Af-Pak strategy debates leave aside the regional stakeholders. Some perfunctory calls have been made to regional players in the shape of an Afghan Contact group and some averments at the London Conference but no substantial cooperation has been sought so far from the regional players.

Over reliance on Pakistan to pull the US and NATO's chestnuts out of the Afghan fire have resulted in the Americans throwing good money after the money gone bad in terms of military and other aid given to Pakistan. Further, Pakistan itself is reeling under multiple terror attacks as a blowback from its failed policies of supporting jihadi terror groups. While Pakistan establishment thinks that it can control Taliban after the departure of western coalition Taliban is more likely to act autonomously throwing more challenges to Pakistan, region and the international community.

It is time for India to consider options other than only soft option of development assistance to Afghanistan. Regional consensus with Iran, Russia, talking to China as also opening backchannels to Pakistan and establishing contacts with important domestic players in Afghanistan is imperative. Guarding against increasing radicalization in Pakistan would another important step. India should also become pro active in defining its core strategic interests in Afghanistan i.e. it should never be allowed to become a haven of terrorists which would embark on a regional or global jihad.